ABORTION IN DEBATE

from John Kennedy

ABORTION IN DEBATE

QUORUM PRESS: EDINBURGH

First published in 1987 by The Saint Andrew Press
on behalf of The Church of Scotland's Board of
Social Responsibility under the Quorum Press imprint,
121 George Street, Edinburgh, EH2 4YN

ISBN 0 86153 094 2

British Library Cataloguing in Publication Data

Abortion in debate – Is there a Christian view?
1. Abortion—Religious aspects—Christianity
I. Church of Scotland. *Board of Social Responsibility*
261.8'3   HQ767.2

ISBN 0-86153-094-2

Typesetting and paste-up by Swanston Graphics Limited, Derby, England
Printed and bound by Bell & Bain Limited, Glasgow, Scotland

Contents

Preface

No issue has been discussed by the Church in recent years with more vigour and strength of feeling than that of abortion. The 1966 Report of the Board of Social Responsibility to the General Assembly of the Church of Scotland carried as one of its headings, 'The Supreme Question' — and for many Christians it is not just another subject of social interest, but the supreme question.

The Report of the Study Group on Abortion of the Board of Social Responsibility was submitted to the General Assembly in 1985 and, after lively and thorough debate, the General Assembly voted in favour of the Deliverance noted in Appendix 1 (p 142).

For the 1986 General Assembly, the Working Party of the Board indicated to the General Assembly that, 'The Study Group on Abortion is continuing its examination of issues raised for the Church by the matter of abortion ... and will report in full to the General Assembly in 1987'. However, after another good debate, the General Assembly voted in favour of the Deliverance noted in Appendix 2 (p 155).

At the 1986 General Assembly, the Board of Social Responsibility intimated that it was commissioning a symposium in which contributors would be asked to express their opinions regarding several relevant aspects of the on-going discussion about abortion. The Board sought advice from some of those who had opposed its original Report, asking them to nominate authors of the various papers. The result is this symposium on abortion. Publication has been delayed because some of those approached were unable, for various reasons, to provide a paper at the time, and because it was arranged that each contributor must be given the opportunity to review and respond to his subject-partner's paper.

The Board of Social Responsibility would like to express gratitude to those who have given of their knowledge and time to contribute to the symposium.

It is the prayer of the Board that the whole Church be encouraged to discuss the symposium — not just the General Assembly nor even Presbyteries, but Kirk Sessions, Woman's Guilds, and Youth Groups — and together study, discuss and pray about this important issue for Christian witness today. Many would say it is 'the Supreme Question' — and questions usually need to be answered.

Frank S Gibson
Secretary and Director of Social Work
Department of Social Responsibility

Notes on Contributors

The Biblical View

Nigel M de S Cameron, MA, (Cantab) BD, PhD
Warden of Rutherford House, Edinburgh, which was established in 1983 as a centre for evangelical study. Dr Cameron has a particular interest in medical ethics. He founded the journal *Ethics and Medicine*, and recently published a book on abortion through Inter-Varsity Press.

Elizabeth Templeton, MA, BD
Formerly lecturer in Philosophy of Religion at New College, Edinburgh. She describes herself currently as 'a freelance theologian', and she recently contributed to the Howard Davis book *Ethics and Medicine*, published by Basil Blackwell.

The Fetus as a Person

Richard A Higginson, BA, (Cantab) MA, PhD
Currently Tutor in Ethics at Cranmer Hall, St John's College, Durham. He is particularly interested in medical ethics and recently wrote Grove Ethics Booklet No 63, *Reply to Warnock*.

Kenneth Boyd, MA, BD, PhD
Scottish Director of the Institute of Medical Ethics. Dr Boyd is Chaplain to Overseas Students at Edinburgh University, and is Associate Minister of St John's and St Cuthbert's Ecumenical Project in Edinburgh.

The Traditional View

Joseph Houston, MA, BD, PhD
Dean of the Faculty of Divinity, University of Glasgow. Dr Houston's main teaching interest is in Systematic Theology and Apologetics.

Ian C M Fairweather, MA, BD
Formerly a Parish Minister in Ayrshire, and lecturer in Religious Education at Jordanhill College of Education, Glasgow. In 1982, was co-author with Dr James I H MacDonald of the book *The Quest for Christian Ethics*. Mr Fairweather is currently Associate Minister at Glasgow Cathedral.

Issues faced by the Medical Profession

J J C Cormack, MD, FRCGP
General Practitioner in the City of Edinburgh who, as a Commissioner to the Church of Scotland General Assembly, has participated in the debates on abortion.

Peter J Armon, FRCOG
Consultant Obstetrician and Gynaecologist with South Cumbria District Health Authority; formerly Consultant with the Kilimanjaro Christian Medical Centre in Tanzania.

Pregnancy Counselling

Nuala Scarisbrick, BA
Honorary Administrator of *LIFE*, in which she has been involved since 1970, and where she councils women about pregnancy.

M Jean Malcolm, COSW
Mrs Malcolm was a Medical Social Worker before she joined the Brook Advisory Centre in 1969 as Organising Secretary. She is presently developing the Brook Educational Programme.

1

Kindness that Kills

The Biblical Perspective on Abortion

The purpose of this essay is three-fold: first, to offer some general remarks on the use of the Bible on such an issue as this one; second, and principally, to indicate the biblical perspective on the practice of abortion; and third, to offer some comments from a biblical point of view on commonly offered grounds for abortion. In an additional note the text in Exodus chapter 21 that is often referred to in this debate is briefly discussed.

How should we set about asking what the Bible has to say about something? We must proceed by way of a number of questions. Is this a modern problem that was unknown in the ancient world? If the answer is yes we must be especially careful. What is the relevance of what the Bible says? That is, does it address the question at the level of principle? Or is it merely an occasional reference? It can also be asked *how* something is argued for in the Bible. Do we meet *ad hominem* argument, or are we dealing with an appeal to fundamental principles?

As is immediately obvious, using the Bible to seek ethical guidance for today can be complex. The complexity of the process does not mean that its conclusions are subjective and therefore unreliable, but it does mean that we must be prepared to follow through a serious argument before we will reach a serious conclusion. It would be naïve to suggest (as some have done) that, because you do not find an entry on 'abortion' in a concordance, the Bible has nothing to say on the subject. Just how naïve that would be will emerge from the discussion which follows.

Abortion in the Ancient World

The Christian attitude to abortion is often approached in the mistaken belief that abortion is something new. It is nothing of the kind. Deliberately induced abortion has been practised in almost all societies, and happens today among

9

primitive peoples as well as in civilised nations. It was particularly common in the Graeco-Roman world, and for much the same reasons as it is common today. Greek society was a permissive society, and women had abortions to cover up illicit relationships and to keep their figures, as well as to limit the size of their families. Of course, it was not without its hazards. But a variety of techniques was developed (including pessaries, drugs and surgery) to make relatively 'safe' termination of pregnancy available.

We should immediately note, however, that not only was abortion a feature of the classical world, but so was opposition to it. Indeed, the best in classical medicine — the Hippocratic tradition that stemmed from the great physician of the fifth century before Christ — was distinctly anti-abortion. The Hippocratic Oath itself makes this clear, and until very recent times the western medical tradition was unwavering in its commitment to this position.

Since this is no new debate, it is in no sense improper for us to seek guidance from the biblical writers if they have guidance to offer.

What then did the Jews and the first Christians make of the practice? They were against it. In a recent study of *Abortion and the Early Church*, commended to the reader by the famous biblical scholar Professor Bruce Metzger, we read the following striking statement:

> It was a given of Jewish thought and life that abortion, like exposure, was unacceptable, and this was well-known in the ancient world....Though rare cases of abortion may have occurred in Judaism, the witness of antiquity is that Jews, unlike pagans, did not practise deliberate abortion.[1]

The first Christians adopted the same position, and the Church maintained it without wavering for many centuries. While there were debates (as there had been in Judaism) about the precise nature of the fetus, in which the embryology of the day and the philosophical notions abroad in the ancient world both featured, Professor Metzger himself is able to comment that, 'It is really remarkable how uniform and how pronounced was the early Christian opposition to abortion'.[2]

What reason did the Christians have — and the Jews before them — for this distinctive stand? They believed that the Old Testament forbade it. So, for example, Josephus, the Jewish writer who was contemporary with the New Testament period, commented that, 'The Law forbids women either to cause abortion or to make away with the fetus'. He continues: 'A woman convicted of this is regarded as an infanticide'.[3] It is of particular interest that this attitude was not confined to the more orthodox of the Jews, but is to be found even among those most heavily influenced by the Greek culture of the day, like Philo. Where there were differences between the Jews — as in later Christian thought — they focused on the legal and personal standing of the fetus, not whether abortion could ever (except for extreme therapeutic reasons) be right. We find, therefore, that the Jews and the early Christians were united in their opposition to abortion, and believed (as Josephus says) that this opposition was Scriptural, despite the fact that nowhere does Scripture forbid abortion in so many words. There are some who would conclude from this that they were mistaken, that they had no right to come to such firm conclusions since they had no evidence for them. The question is *how* they came to them, or, more importantly, how we — if we follow in their footsteps — may ourselves come to such conclusions.

The Major Question Today

The ancient condemnation of abortion by Jews and Christians alike could not be on the ground that this text or the Old Testament condemned it as a distinctive practice, because they do not. Rather, its condemnation was considered to be implicit in the prohibition of murder. If such a conclusion is valid for us today it is necessary that two propositions should be established:

(1) Human life is sacred — *ie* that (apart from the widely recognised exceptional reasons of judicial execution and just warfare) it is always wrong to kill a human being.

(2) The life of the child before birth is 'human life' in such a sense as to bring it within the scope of that principle.

For the purposes of this discussion we shall assume that the first of these principles is accepted. It has, of course, been challenged, notably in the cases of handicapped new-born children and the elderly. Many (including some Christians) have argued that their lives are not to be protected, and that in some circumstances doctors can kill. But that is a broader question, and the killing of elderly people and handicapped children remains the crime of murder. It is not so with the killing of children before they are born.

It is widely believed that the evidence for a specifically *biblical* case against abortion is weak. This is partly because Christian opponents of abortion have sometimes used weak arguments. There has been a tendency to over-emphasise texts which properly have more of a supporting role to play, and a failure to exploit some major theological arguments.

There are two fundamental Christian doctrines which may be brought to bear on this question by reason of their implications for the biblical understanding of human life before birth. They are none less than the doctrines of Creation and Incarnation.

Creation

The fundamental fact that the Bible teaches about man is that he is made in the 'image of God'. We do not know the extent to which man 'images' God, but the chief role played by this fact in Scripture is in lending weight to the dignity and worth of the life of man. This is evident especially in Genesis 9, where we read that the life of man is sacred *because* God made man in his image (Gen. 9:6).

It needs to be emphasised that the image of God does not involve any special moral or religious *qualities* in the one who bears it, beyond those which are common to all the race. Man *as such* bears the image, not 'this man' or 'that man'. It cannot be forfeited, and there is no man nor woman who does not share in this basic fact which is part and parcel of being creatures of God.

What then of the child before birth? The Bible makes no distinction. The image does not depend upon any particular quality or ability; it is something which is imparted to man in general. This is made plain in Genesis chapter 1 where we find a taxonomy of the created order.

We read of the fish, the birds, the animals, the plants — and *man*; man as a species, *Homo sapiens* as we now call him. It is *man* who is created 'in the image of God'.

That may seem a simple statement, but its implications are profound. Wherever we find man — man as opposed to beast or bird — we find one who bears the image of God. There are implications also, of course, for the dignity of women, for as members of the species along with men they bear the divine image too. There are implications for racial questions, since here there is no distinction between Jew and Gentile, white and black. There are implications for the physically and mentally handicapped, since they too are members with us of a common human race: there is no 'quality control' here which might suggest that the deformed or sub-normal are denied the supreme dignity of the image of their Maker. And there are implications too for those human beings, members with us of a common species, who happen not yet to have been born. They too are 'man', fellow-members of the human race, constituted genetically like us from the very beginning. The image of God extends to humankind wherever the race is to be found.

In practical terms the importance of this principle will be seen in the examples which history provides of the arbitrary denial of fully human character to certain classes of those who are undoubtedly human beings. In less enlightened times the mentally retarded and the mentally ill were treated like animals, and the physically deformed (like the Elephant Man whose story was recently filmed to such powerful effect) were exploited as circus exhibits. Under the Third Reich, the Jews were classed as non-persons, so they had no protection from abuse and finally from destruction. Under the system of apartheid today, the skin-colour of people has become the determinant of their civil rights and their human dignity. The common factor in each of these cases is the arbitrary principle that something other than the biological fact that this-is-a-member-of-the-human-species has come to be allowed to determine the dignity and personal worth of the subject. It is exactly the same with the unborn.

The Bible extends the infinite dignity and consequent protection of the image of God to every member of the human species. That is the significance for our discussion of its first chapter. Mankind as such bears the image of its Maker.

One further comment is necessary here. It is sometimes suggested that the bearing of the image of God is connected with some specific quality or capability in man. Yet every quality and capability which has been proposed (such as artistic creativity or the ability to engage in relationships) is evidently lacking, not simply in the unborn (who in any event begin to develop in such directions before they are born in a way that is directly continuous with their life in the months which follow birth), but in those who come to biological maturity while mentally deficient. Unless they too are regarded as sub-humans, from whom the image of God is withheld, such a suggestion cannot stand scrutiny. In any event, the biblical text itself implies that the image, far from being something which develops in human experience, is in fact part of the 'given' of human life. So we read, 'In the image of God *has God made man*' (Gen.9:6, New English Bible). It is part of the essential make-up of man — indeed, it is this which actually *constitutes* man, being ontologically inseparable from those biological/genetic factors which distinguish him from the other orders of creation.

Incarnation
The doctrine of the incarnation is as central to the Christian faith as that of the creation. God who made man has also *become* man, without ceasing to be God.

God became man in the way in which we become men, first of all *as a child*. To be more precise, the gestation of a human child was the vehicle by which incarnation was brought about. This is the testimony of the birth narratives recorded in the New Testament and it has been a central conviction of the Church, enshrined in the credal affirmation that Jesus Christ was 'conceived by the Holy Ghost, born of the Virgin Mary'.

The implications of this are obvious. If we ask — as many ask — 'When does human life begin?, there is an answer in the human life of our Lord. Our uncertainty as to when *our* human lives begin — that is, as to whether they are conterminous with the biological life of unborn children — can be answered with reference to the beginning of our Lord's life. This is so for two reasons. The first of which is because his is a particular human life whose beginnings are recorded in Scripture in some detail. It is sometimes retorted that his human life was an exception, that his was a human life 'unlike ours in every way'.[5] The answer to this question leads us to the second reason: the human life of our Lord was not *simply* a particular human life, it was a typical, representative human life. The biblical teaching is that it was like ours in every way except in one respect — that it was sinless. His life *had to be like ours* in every other respect, or he could not have redeemed us. To be our Redeemer, he had to be one of us, and the Church has rejected any lesser view as heresy. In particular the life of the man Jesus Christ cannot be separated from the life of the Son of God. They are not two separate people, but the life of Jesus *is* the human life of God. This is underscored by the belief in the eternal humanity of Jesus Christ. Having once taken on human form, God has not laid it down.

Therefore the manner in which the incarnate Son experienced human existence not only may but *must* be seen as a paradigm of all human existence. And there can be no doubt that his human life, in the sense of his personal and moral identity, began at the point of the virginal conception in the womb of his mother. This can be established exegetically from the narrative in Luke (1:34–35, New English Bible) where a particular point is spoken of: ᵢhe Holy Spirit 'came upon' her, and the 'power of the Most High ... overshadowed' her, in the miraculous moment of conception.

In the case of the Son of God himself this has momentous implications. It identifies the point of incarnation in space and time not with his birth but with his earliest origins. Not in a cradle merely has God deigned to be 'contracted to a span', but in the microscopic dimensions of a fertilised ovum. The perilous human existence of the incarnate Son began not in his birth under threat from Herod, but in the hazardous journey of a days-old embryo from out of his mother's Fallopian tubes to seek safe lodgement in the wall of her uterus.

The reason why the incarnation sheds such light on human personal origins is simple. In this case, and in this case alone, we face a person who had a pre-history, a pre-existence. He was not a new personal being, but a personal existence. There could therefore be no ambiguity about his own origin as a human person since it was not only his origin but also the point at which he acted in a particular way. 'The Word *became* flesh', we read in John 1:14 but he already 'was', from the beginning. The identification of his 'becoming flesh' with the mode of his mother's conception demonstrates conclusively the personal nature and capacity of the early embryo.

Such a conclusion is amply borne out by the details of the Gospel birth narratives. Elizabeth greets her cousin Mary, who is at a very early stage of her pregnancy, with the question, 'Why am I so favoured, that *the mother of my Lord* should come to me?' (Luke 1:43, New International Version). Further, the word used for 'baby' throughout this narrative is *brephos*, which does indeed mean 'baby' (it is later used by Luke for the new-born Jesus and also for the children brought to him for blessing, 2:12, 18:15, NEB). Again, and of considerable significance, we note that Elizabeth is carrying her own son, John, at around six months' gestation and that we have just read that she has felt him leap in her womb 'for joy' (1:41, 44), fulfilling the promise of the angel that he will be filled with the Holy Spirit from his mother's womb' (1:15). The fact that the author of this Gospel is widely believed to have been a physician adds significance to the details of the narrative.

Supporting Arguments
There are two further arguments which may be brought in to support these major doctrinal considerations.

First, the biblical significance of the act of begetting — human life is seen as transmitted not at birth but in the procreative act itself. Considerable portions of the Bible are taken up with genealogical lists, and they take the form 'Abraham begat Isaac'. The point at which Abraham began to have posterity was the point of the begetting of his son, the start of Isaac's life *in utero*. There is no suggestion that any later point in the life of the unborn child should be regarded as of any significance in this respect.

Second, there are many illustrations in the Old Testament in which the life of the unborn child is reflected upon from later life. It is these examples which have been seized upon by opponents of abortion, and they certainly have a part to play, although as we have indicated there are arguments at a more fundamental level which have prior place. Several of the psalms take up this theme, particularly Psalm 139, and there are a number of passages in the prophets and in Job with a similar subject. Some of these texts, at least, logically require the continuity of personal life inside and outside the womb for their meaning to stand. For example:

> May [the Lord] hear wailing in the morning,
>   a battle cry at noon.
> For he did not kill me in the womb,
>   with my mother as my grave,
>   her womb enlarged for ever.
> Why did I ever come out of the womb
>   to see trouble and sorrow
>   and to end my days in shame?
>
> (Jeremiah 20:16*b*–18, NIV)

Or, again:

> Why then did you bring me out of the womb?
>   I wish I had died before any eye saw me.
> If only I had never come into being,
>   or had been carried straight from the womb
>   to the grave!
>
> (Job 10:18–19, NIV)

Not only is personal continuity asserted in these and other passages, with multiple usage of the first personal pronoun, but there are specific logical implications in some of them, including the one cited from Job 10. Job is contrasting two possibilities which clearly require to be dissimilar: that he had never come into being, or that he had been stillborn. The implication is plain, in that the still-born child has already had a personal existence before it dies.

The Biblical Position

It is therefore evident that the absence of a specific prohibition of induced abortion in Holy Scripture is of no special relevance to the discussion. The taking of human life is forbidden, and human life that is morally significant is held to be conterminous with the biological life of man. The *imago Dei* attaches to man at every stage of his existence and in every form that it takes. Not only is emphasis laid on the continuity of life before and after birth, but the personal life of the unborn child is demonstrated in the incarnation *in utero* of the Son of God.

Indeed the arguments which we have elaborated from creation and incarnation come together at this point, since it is because man bears the divine image that incarnation is made possible. God can become man because man was made like God. The incarnation of the Son of God in the form of a human embryo is possible because already at this most primitive stage in human existence man bears the divine image. Conversely, if even at such a stage human life can be taken up into the life of God, we see the inordinate dignity and infinite value which that life already bears.

It is no wonder that explicit repudiation of induced abortion needed no place in the canon of sacred Scripture, since it was inherently impossible to harmonise with everything else that they believed. Both the Jews and the first Christians were compelled to abjure abortion and stand against the fashionable tide of opinion of their day. If the Church of our own day desires to take a biblical view on the matter it has no option but to follow them.

Arguments for Abortion

We have presented the lineaments of the biblical case against abortion, founded not on isolated texts, nor on legislation that might be time-bound, but on fundamental, doctrinal considerations which entail a view of intra-uterine life as personally human. There are some who would share in much, perhaps in all, of this reasoning; who would accept its theological conclusions; and yet who would deny that this must lead to a principled opposition to the practice of abortion.

There are several possible causes of such a position. Generally there is insufficient attention to the significance of the arguments which are being adduced. It is, of course, also possible to hold that, in principle, human life is not sacred; so that to establish fetal life as full human life is not to establish its sanctity. More often there is the strange idea that, valid though these arguments may be, the choice of the lesser evil, or the requirements of the pluralistic society, place curbs upon our application of such principles to practice. But, while the application of principles is often complex — if the thesis that fetal life is human life in the image of God is accepted — it is hard to see how a Christian who made any claim to consistency could then go on to approve induced abortion outside a life-saving context.

There is only one value which is equivalent to that of a human life, and that is another human life. Whatever other benefits may be held to accrue from the killing of a fetus — and, of course, there can be many — only the saving of another human life provides a value of the same order to set in the scale against the deed that must be done.[6]

It may be helpful in conclusion to survey some of the alleged grounds for abortion from this perspective, and to comment briefly upon each.

Congenital Handicap
Screening techniques have made it possible to diagnose various fetal abnormalities during pregnancy, with a view to aborting the babies found to be defective. Curiously, many Christians regard this as a particularly compelling argument for abortion. In fact it sets the biblical notion of compassion upon its head, taking a eugenic, quality-control approach to human life which is the antithesis of the biblical concern for the handicapped and diseased. Our Lord's ministry is one of healing and compassion, and behind the Church's following in that ministry lies confidence in the resurrection of the dead, when the lame man shall leap as a hart, and the tongue of the dumb shall sing. It is difficult not to find the aborting of handicapped babies uniquely abhorrent. If anything could be worse it is the context in which this is sometimes done, when there is known to be a possibility of genetic disorder and a woman undergoes regular screening, with perhaps a series of abortions while she awaits the birth of a 'normal' child. The Christian does not kill those who suffer or are defective.

Rape
This is of course the most emotive of all grounds for abortion, since, in those rare cases in which pregnancy follows, the woman having suffered an appalling attack now finds herself bearing the child of her attacker. Yet the child is also her own, perhaps the only child she will ever bear. And the child is innocent, a third party. The Bible teaches forgiveness and the protection of the innocent. The idea that the child should die for the sin of its father is itself obnoxious, but there is more to be said. Will this further assault really benefit the mother? It cannot undo the dreadful thing that has been done to her by denying her motherhood even as the rapist has denied her womanhood.

Other Grounds

A variety of social grounds are alleged for abortion.[7] It cannot be doubted that many children are conceived in circumstances of stress and poverty, in which the possibility of ending the pregnancy has great attractions both for the mother and also for the professionals who are seeking to help her. Whether she is a student mid-way through a course, or already has several children and cannot cope with another, or if perhaps she has been deserted by the child's father, it is of no advantage to play down the grave difficulties which she might face. But are they sufficient reasons to argue for the taking of a human life? And is it *ever* in the interests of a mother for her child to be killed in order to solve a problem?[8]

It is difficult not to conclude, in each of these cases, that once the principle is admitted that abortion would not prevent the pregnancy since the mother *already has* a child, the interests of mother and child coincide in the continuation of the pregnancy to term, perhaps in special accommodation, and — in some cases — with the birth followed by adoption.

Additional Note: Exodus 21:22–25

This text has been used by Christian writers on the subject of abortion (such as R F R Gardner in *Abortion: The Personal Dilemma*[8] because it is claimed to be the only biblical text which addresses the issue of abortion directly. But it does nothing of the sort. It deals not with induced abortion but with miscarriage. The exact meaning of the text is uncertain. It speaks of a brawl between two men in which a pregnant woman is accidentally struck and caused to give birth. The RSV reads (21:22): 'When men strive together, and hurt a woman with child, so that there is a miscarriage, and yet no harm follows, the one who hurt her shall be fined.' On the other hand, 'If any harm follows', there shall be a reckoning of 'life for life' (v.23).

This can be taken in two different ways. The question is, 'If harm follows', then to whom? If the child is left out of the account and the mother only is in view, it is said that the text implies a low view of fetal life, since only a fine is levied (no 'life for life'). So people like Mr Gardner have argued that this text justifies induced abortion. But even on that reading it does not. Since the miscarriage is produced by accident (the man did not attack the mother, still less try to *induce* the miscarriage) the punishment is given for producing a miscarriage by reckless brawling in the presence of a pregnant woman. The fact that it is a fine should not make us think it is meant to be trivial (like a fine can be today), since the choice lay between a fine and physical punishment, there being no imprisonment in ancient Israel.

What is more, the passage occurs immediately after another which discusses the penalty for beating a slave to death. The question of slavery is a complex one. It is sufficient to say that the penalty set out is much less severe than that for killing a free man, and yet someone like Mr Gardner would not claim that the Bible does *not* teach the *full humanity* of the slave.

Moreover, another interpretation is possible, and has much to support it. 'If harm follows', may include the child as well as the mother. Given the view of the unborn child taken in the rest of the Bible this is antecedently more likely). In that case the 'life for life' penalty would apply if the child dies as a result of premature delivery.

Whichever interpretation is placed on this passage, it does not provide any support for the view that before birth the child is less than a full human being. And on one interpretation it would strongly support the view we have taken up in this essay.[9]

Notes to Paper 1

1   Michael J Gorman, *Abortion and the Early Church* (Downers Grove, Illinois, 1982), pp 33f.

2   ibid, p 9.

3   *Against Apion* ii 202, cited by G J Wenham, 'A Biblical Theologian looks at Abortion' in *Abortion: The Biblical and Medical Challenges* (London, 1983).

4   Another way of expressing this argument is to say that it is up to the biologist to determine what is a human being and what is not. That is the objective quality which this discussion brings to the debate. It is not up to the ethicist, nor the exegete, and ethical and exegetical arguments which seek another road need first to get round the logic of this position.

5   This question was put in these very words to the present writer in a recent radio interview.

6   This is not intended to imply any particular view of the relative priority of fetal and maternal life; only that in a case where maternal life is actually threatened, a case could be made for the taking of fetal life which was not both immoral and, logically speaking, absurd. We simply do not contemplate killing people for other reasons if we claim to be reasonable men and women.

7   It is of course true that *all* grounds for abortion are 'social' grounds. The only actual 'therapeutic' ground (*ie* which promotes health and healing) is in the case of risk to the mother's life, in which case any abortion is only a by-product of 'therapeutic' treatment of the mother. Much of the vocabulary of this debate has been twisted to make the killing of unborn children seem respectable, when it can never be other than sordid.

8   These and other questions of detail are discussed more fully in *Abortion: The Crisis in Morals and Medicine,* by the present writer and Pamela F Sims, FRCS, MRCOG (Leicester, 1986).

9   R F R Gardner, *Abortion: The Personal Dilemma* (Exeter, 1972).

10   There is a fuller discussion in *Abortion: The Crisis in Morals and Medicine,* Appendix 2, where references are given to technical treatments.

2

Abortion: Our Painful Freedom

The Theological Setting

The division between Christians of good faith concerning abortion emerges from a difference in theology. It is not, that is to say, primarily a biological debate about when life starts. Nor is it about whether the taking of life among human beings is part of the manifest pain and brokenness of belonging in a 'fallen' world. Rather it is about our basic vision of how God relates to us in that world, how much freedom we believe we are given under him to affect the lives and deaths of our fellows, how the Church is called to manifest his new Kingdom while embedded in a world still visibly unhealed although to faith redeemed.

Connected with that vision, there is a difference in fairly basic understanding and use of Scripture. It is not just that different visions of God are partly formed by how Scripture is read and interpreted; but also that the way of reading and interpreting is affected by the expectation of *how* God works in the world: and that in itself is conditioned by religious and secular culture, Church tradition, and other factors which are often so taken for granted as to go unnoticed and uncommented on. So, for instance, Christians who *expect* blow-by-blow directions from God as to how they should behave *assume* that Scripture will offer guidance in certain ways, say by affirming absolute general principles, or by providing immediately transferable values from biblical situations to present ones. Christians, on the other hand, who *assume* that God gives them much more rope and scope to explore the world, not under tutelage, do not expect that sort of guidance. Rather they find in Scripture a key manifestation of that human exploration of the constant love of God, disclosed in one tract of Middle-Eastern history. That interaction between disclosure and exploration is held as revelatory, as something which clarifies and challenges all human existence; yet it is not seen as providing a blueprint of immediate divine directives about contemporary dilemmas.

The debate then, within the Churches — and that is only part of the debate — is not, except in its most distorted vulgarisations, between Christians who

20

believe in the absolute authority of God and those Christians who do not. It is not between Christians who accept the authority of the Bible and Christians who do not. It is not between Christians who accept the sanctity of life and Christians who do not. It is not between Christians who compromise with liberal secularism and Christians who do not. It is about different visions of God, of salvation and of responsive Christian life.

So, the Christian story goes, God loved into being a world which did not need to be there for any other reason than his love. There was no necessity internal or external for God to create it, nor was the world part of God's being. It was a quite new thing, made out of nothing by God's potent, imaginative love. Because it was made out of nothing, not out of God, the world was significantly 'other'. That in part constituted its goodness in God's sight: He did not determine it, or control it. He went for walks out of the garden! But also because it was made out of nothing, it was precarious. If it lost its open relatedness to the God who gave it life, it was liable to disintegration and to death.

The axis of this precarious freedom was the human person who was to emerge from the complexity of organic life — the Adam of biblical myth. It was the creative intention of God that persons would in freedom steward the earth in response to his own love and freedom, and would sustain its transformation towards life in his presence.

Woman/man however found all this too menacing a promise and possibility. For if all their being and knowing was to be involved with the life of God, then their taped, manageable and mastered world would explode into new and amazing strangeness. Their own identity would not be confined to their natural, safe and self-sustaining groupings, in family, clan, class, nation; for living in the constant presence of God, they would be opened up to a more generous identification — with, for example, the marginal, the deviant, the outsider, 'the other', the preferably ignored. Their ethics would be disrupted, for they could no longer define and classify people by their pasts, by their merits or demerits. For the invitation of God is to 'underline' people by their future, to know them in the open hiddenness of what will become of them in God.

So woman/man preferred to stay in a controllable world, where they could apparently contain and defuse the explosive presence of God — and they ate of the fruit of the knowledge of good and evil, which was tragically available in the absence of God; for he would not violate the freedom he had conferred, by loving people into his presence with superior baits of power, knowledge or necessity.

That is one reading of the haunting and distinctive narrative which Jews and Christians share as the story of the Fall: it is not for many Christians readable as a causal, historical account, but it maps out some existential connections between, say, our will to manage and define our identity in protected, intact circles, and the multiple unsatisfactoriness and brokenness of things — our umpteen moral failures, the blurring of our vision of God, the cosmic and cosmological tragedies which beset us, the presence of death, the constraints of time, space and causality which menace us as free beings, our 'embeddedness' in contexts and structures which frustrate our openness to the future, and to the newness of God.

The New Testament maps another interaction between God and the human person, one centred on the person Jesus, who recreates the situation, identifies God (in the person of his Son) with the broken and precarious world, and by costly stewarding reworks creation's response and redefines our selfhood, representing God's creative intention in freedom.

In the light of that act of God, as the response it generated, there is the Church, the token of a transformed creation, called to signal to the world the reality and hope of its future in Christ to confess the past and present we define ourselves by, and to offer the taste of his Kingdom in word, sacrament and life.

This is then, I believe, the context of the abortion debate, as Christians distinctively contribute to it. We may of course discuss it in all sorts of other terms, overlapping with other ideological positions. We could focus on the question of 'right' of the mother, or of the community — but this seems to me liable to distort the discussion from the outset. For it isolates and polarises, and sets in competition, at least potentially, elements of a situation which can be appreciated only as an interconnected fabric. There is of course something of vital importance indicated by the language of 'rights' of the fetus — namely that what is a potential person cannot be discarded like a piece of litter. There is also something of vital importance indicated by talking of the 'rights' of the mother; about the vocation and destiny of any woman in a specific situation. But *who* either the fetus or the mother *is* depends on many complex and interwoven elements. It is certainly true that Christianity has contributed to the human sense of the irreplaceability of the person, against ideologies of collectivism or totalitarianism. Nevertheless, that irreplaceability is not, it seems to me, the absolute individualism which Western European ideology has made it, but an irreplaceability within relationship, where persons are made or unmade not by sheer existence, but by love, as God is made in the mutuality of Father, Son and Spirit.

Once you insist that personhood is relational, the fetus, the mother, the family, the community, all become open and fluid identities, not unreal, but mutually interdependent, and defined not by biology or by sociology, but by love, by uncoerced relationship. (How often does the New Testament challenge the centrality of biology in defining kinship for instance, and is that more rhetoric? Who are my father, my mother, my brothers, my neighbours?) What it means, if it means anything, in a distinctively Christian sense, to respect persons, cannot be reduced to an ethic of individual rights. That rationalises and schematises the interconnectedness of our human existence, and the tension between the generous co-existence of the Kingdom and the limited co-existence we are capable of in a dying world.

Let us move then from that theological preamble to the question of how Christians responsibly face the critical dilemma about abortion. I would like to press the question by presenting a number of theses which seem to me, if not proven, at least plausible in the light of the foregoing theology. If any particular thesis falls, the theological case for abortion as a defensible action by Christians in good faith is weakened, although not necessarily defeated. If the theses stand, then a Christian case for abortion as permissible and sometimes justified is made.

1 *The chance and necessity which result in conception are not to be equated with the will of God.*
It is a kind of fatalism, more related to pagan determinism or Islam to assume that everything which happens naturally is the will of God. (Calvinism is the strand of Christianity most liable to this distortion and it overshadows Scottish piety for ill.) If the doctrine of the Fall is to be taken seriously, God is not equidistantly behind everything which happens in the world. Nature and God may be at odds. Aspects of the natural world may frustrate as well as manifest the love and freedom which are God's creative hope for it. The birth of severely deformed children (or for that matter childlessness) *may be* such aspects. We are not allowed to indulge in the theological cosmic Toryism of 'whatever is, is right'.

2 *Particularly if we accept that conception and contraception have become responsibilities delegated to us, rather than an accident of fate or a dictate of Providence; if in fact we believe that Providence opens up our responsibility, we can no longer assume that conception is, of itself, good, whatever the circumstances.*
This is, of course, a theologically and socially divisive issue. The current doctrine and official practice of the Roman Catholic Church insists on distinguishing between legitimate 'natural' and illegitimate 'artificial' methods of birth control. This position implies: (a) the equation we have questioned above, *ie* of God's will with nature, and (b) that all methods of interfering with natural processes are wrong, even before a fetus is formed — *eg* sterilisation, vasectomy, use of contraceptive pills, and so on.
  Many Christians accept that artificial modes of contraception are one of the emerging tools of our adult responsibility: not that we have wrested power

from God, but that this outcome of scientific and medical research may be held as a gift, and used. If we believe that God allows us to plan when sexual activity will lead to conception, and particularly if we accept methods of contraception which prevent implantation after conception (*eg* the coil), it is not a consistent ground for refusing abortion that it resists and defies the natural process.

It is, of course, a long way from saying that contraception is permissible to saying that abortion is. However, one 'nihil obstat' is cleared if we believe that *decisions* about conception are meant to be ours; and that contraceptive failure must not be taken as the backlash of fate or in the intervention of God.

3 *If we deny that post-conceptial contraception is a proper responsibility of human beings, and see it as a violation of our obedience to providence, we must of course consistently refuse abortion. But we are then responsible for handling a future which involves the progressive doubling of the world's population every generation, and generates, indirectly, other forms of death for living people.*

Is it a specifically Christian vision of the world that we should, without limit, be fruitful and multiply? This conviction depends on a view of God whose recommendations are unchanging and unchangingly interpreted through all historical context. The Semitic Old Testament context of this confidence about settlement and fertility could not possibly have envisaged the world of our ecological projections, exhaustible resources, urban distress, famine and global competition for space, land and survival. If our Christian response is, 'That's God's business, he will provide', we are being highly selective about our non-interventions. Why do we not rule out surgical interventions or famine relief operations, and assume that the providence of God will take over?

4 *Abortion is, in some cases, the only viable way of avoiding human consequences anticipated as more disastrous than the death of the fetus.*

There are situations, tragically, in which people say, 'It would have been better if I had never been born'. We cannot, of course, anticipate this: finding that it is so is a risk which human beings may choose to take, or may find themselves incapable of facing. If it seems clear, say within the nuclear family, that a child will be born so grossly deformed or in such constant pain that its life will be unrelievedly distressed, and its family's life broken irreparably, or if it is clear within a nation (say China or India?) that the unrestricted multiplication of children will produce in the foreseeable future disastrous pressure on ungrowing resources, then conception once it happens, through accident or carelessness, is already a disaster. The provision of care, adequate to a human life, either on the microcosmic or macrocosmic scale, is not a foreseeable possibility within the family, community, society in question. This is not to deny that it is tragic that the abortion is found necessary, but it may be the responsibly judged lesser of two evils.

5 *There is no absolute theological basis for the assertion that life is, at all costs, to be saved. If that is offered as the axiom which justifies surgical intervention or famine relief, and outlaws abortion, we are utterly hypocritical and inconsistent in the other ethical stances we historically condone, which relativise the taking of life to other values.*

We live, as a Western European Church in a context which commits us on the whole without self-criticism, to the systematic, if slow and unobtrusive, killing of people in the Third World. We endorse a political system which is committed in the last resort to the extermination of nations judged hostile to our freedom, faith or ideology (*viz* the Warsaw pact countries which are the target of our nuclear capacity) and to the probable mutual destruction of our own culture, the world's ecosystem and the future of life on this planet. If life as such is relativised by the values on which such 'Christianly' sanctioned decisions are based, it is sheer cant to be absolutists about the abortion issue (*cf* the question of judicial execution and its warrants).

6 *If it is granted that the taking of life is seen as sometimes a responsible option for human beings in a broken world, then the abortion issue becomes one, not of absolute rights and wrongs, but like most ethical issues, of the relative merits and demerits of letting a child be born in a situation where its life is likely to be, or to cause, an overwhelming experience of negativity within the world it will concretely inhabit.*

Of course, ideally, we might hope the acute distress and isolation of serious mental or physical handicap would not exist to deform the beauty and freedom of human beings. Even in a marginally better world, where congenital damage and viral disease to the fetus still existed, one can envisage a human world where the resources of the whole community were committed to supporting and offering creative help to those with handicapped children, and to the children themselves. That is not, on the whole, the state of our world. Although there are outstanding instances of loving creativity where a family manages to find blessing in the life of a severely deformed child, this cannot be made a norm. There are, psychologically and sociologically, far more cases where families are wrecked, emotionally and sometimes physically, by the nightmare strain of watching and caring for a child in constant pain and impotence. It is not, of course, a matter of headcounting. The possibility of responsible abortion cannot be generalised into a prescription, nor can its prohibition. It belongs to that delicate area of responsible choice which might, in Christian terms be called vocation, where those involved have to assess, in fear and trembling, their own capacity to cope.

7 *The prediction of negativity is not, of course, an absolute, if we believe in the transcendent creativity of God; but the transformation of overwhelming and destructive pain is not guaranteeable, and we are not entitled to prescribe heroic faith to other people.*

There are, of course, prodigious and conspicuous examples of such transformations — Beethoven overcoming deafness, Helen Keller overcoming multiple disability, and so on. But we cannot guarantee that God will swoop in to rescue us from our destructive experiences, any more than he will magically block our political lunacies, self neglect and human ineptitude. We may believe in his promises of rescue and restoration, but the future of the Kingdom is not always manifest, and we are here and now faced with the dilemma of how to plan responsible co-existence on the assumption that the probabilities of natural causality will operate. It is an act of heroic and Christlike faith to trust that God will transform situations of immense pain and stress into creative possibilities. It cannot be taken for granted that people are capable of that, and certainly it cannot be prescribed as a response by a Church which lives as much by prudent self-conservation as by heroic faith.

8 *The Church's proper response to the incapacity of the world to be its eschatologically conditioned self is not to assume a positive of superior morality, but to share and represent the passion of its Lord, who suffered and identified himself with all the ambiguity and negativity of the human situation.*

It is doubtful whether in any case there is an ethic proper to the Kingdom of God, any more than there is an ethic belonging to the life of God himself. For the Kingdom of God is that condition of existence where there is such integrated and undivided life that no constraint operates, and no agonies of divisive decision are to be encountered. If the Church is to be witness to that post-ethical community of a new earth, it misinterprets that vocation by trying to impose the conditions of eschatology on to a pre-eschatological world. Even if the Church were strong enough in faith to insist that *all* life can be sustained and cherished in the light of God's love, it cannot make a law out of its Gospel by insisting that people should be forced to cope with the nurture of children they are unwilling to have, and incapable of offering a valued and recognisably human life. Of course, if the Church is willing to shoulder the nurture of children who might otherwise have been aborted, this might open the option of letting such children survive: but the responsibility must be sustainable beyond infancy and even beyond childhood, and there is no evidence that either the Churches or the community are able and willing to meet the immense additional strain on resources, generosity of care and alternative structures of nurturing. It is then understandable and not to be judged 'from above' that people should decide with painful realism that the only manageable long-term solution is abortion. This involves the planned destruction of a person, or a potential person, which is clearly an awful responsibility: but it is no more awful than many of the responsibilities we shoulder as adults in a world such as we inhabit. We are not, as the Church is, immunised from the pain or the sinfulness of such human predicaments, but we are invited to 'sin boldly', not in pride or complacency at our decisions, but in confidence that God himself suffers with us in all the ambiguity of our imperfect choices. Ethics, as Bonhoeffer constantly points out, must not cancel our humanness, as if we were translated into a divine 'safe zone' where we left sin behind.

9 *It is naïve and ungenerous of the Church to make general ethical statements against abortion which ignore the political loading of such pressure against the poor.*
God affirms his love of the whole world. Yet contemporary theology and mission recognise that the prophets, and Jesus himself, constantly focus that love in terms of solidarity with the poor; a theological ethic which, in effect, is not intentional, is loaded against the poor, and which distorts the Gospel.

Any ecclesiastical veto on abortion, and certainly any more restrictive legislation would certainly be so loaded. The rich and sophisticated will always be able to manage smooth and safe abortions. It is those at the bottom of the social heap, without the escape circuits of the rich, least able to cope with unwanted pregnancy and additional children, who will in fact be forced again into back street abortions, with all their dire medical and social consequences.

Ethical proclamations, intended as universal, which fail to register the actual social and psychological probabilities within a given context mark a theological failure. For they falsify the specific evangelical concern that the love of God be earthed in special responsiveness to the plight of the poor.

10 *Christian energy and concern about abuses of our present legislation would be more constructively channelled into maximising the chance of genuinely, not just formally, responsible decision-making among those involved.*
The intention of the present act was to provide for humane and considered judgement that the carrying of a fetus to term would, in all probability, create a worse human situation for all involved than its termination. For some Christians that judgement could never be made, but for others, as for many of different faiths, ideologies or commitments, it sometimes is made, and is endorsed even by doctors vocationally motivated and strongly trained to save life.

Rather than using its political energies to crusade for legislation imposing a limited theological perspective on a pluralistic society, the Church would be better advised to facilitate the kind of encounter which would actually increase the level of responsibility in the decision-making. People are often isolated by panic, stress or pressure of time as they approach the dilemma about abortion. We would better express the love of God by working for structures which break down that isolation, and let those affected become aware of the many layers of medical, social, political, ethical and religious concern involved. We would also reflect better the fact of God entrusting us to adulthood, and his response to the world's fallenness being one of involvement rather than censorious dissociation.

The thrust of this argument has been that the need for abortion arises in a fallen world such as this is, where it is tragically not true that all new life, meant in creation as a gift and delight, can be received and sustained in that way. It seems to me no service to the pro-abortionist case to try to wriggle out of the gravity of the human problem, by aiming to prove that the fetus is a mere thing, within the automatic right of the mother to dispose of. It has the potential for life (given certain conditions of nurture), although so have sperm and ova given certain conditions of nurture, and no one expresses any theological or biological distress about the interruption of those potentials, and the prodigal waste of sperm and ova!

This is not to be happy or complacent about the need for abortion. It is, however, the drawing of a theological map in which the actual character of our broken, often dehumanised, world is taken as seriously as the incarnation takes it. It is not an issue between facile laissez-faire permissiveness and Christian integrity. It is a question of how Christian integrity manifests itself, and of facing the complexities and conflicts *within* the Christian community about how it understands God, freedom, responsibility, sin, forgiveness, and the Church's role in a pluralist society.

Of course we face a problem.

I am convinced that the Church's right to make public statements on the abortion issue has to be affirmed: but that it loses credibility if it fails to face up to the complexity of its own motivation and response. How far is its primary concern the sanctity of life, and how far is it unexplored terror at living in a world which faces us with life and death decisions which the Church would rather avoid by referring to absolute authority of some sort? How far are we the heirs of a Christian tradition which has been strong on ethical pronouncements which are aimed at individuals (particularly on sexually-related issues — promiscuity, permissiveness, and so on), but has ignored planks of socio-political culpability in its own eye? Has the Church even begun to face up to the theological and ethical pluralism within it, as a preliminary to maintaining the larger catholicity of being human?

If the Church is truly an incarnational community, it is not allowed to, and should not be capable of, dissociating itself from some less moral 'them' — a sub-group of human beings on whom the fallenness of the world is blamed, or in whose attitudes and practices it is located. The wretchedness of a world (microcosmic or macrocosmic) which cannot cope with unlimited more children, which cannot altogether organise itself into contraceptive efficiency, which is thoroughly unjust in the distribution of resources for adequate, let alone full, life, is the wretchedness of the world *we* have made and are invested in. It is not then for us to stand aside as if we could have morally clean hands by saying, 'Let all fetuses go on living'. We are already involved in the fallenness of things. We should at least have the courage to be frank about our often terrifying freedom to make life and death decisions. For let us not deceive ourselves. If we decide as a society to restrict or refuse abortion, we are still making life and death decisions, but differently distributed and less able to be mapped out in terms of those who suffer the outcome.

The Church is properly called to confess our distance from the worlds of Eden and Paradise from the new humanness of Christ to which we are invited. We are called too, to manifest the new kind of community we hope to become, where 'unwanted child' would be a contradiction in terms, and where even the awful distress of a family with congenitally diseased children might be transformed by unfailing support and creative care. But until we can offer that, concretely, our central affirmation must be that as we participate in the messiness, pain and frustration of an untransformed world, we are held and involved in the love and foregiveness of God.

That is not, I hope, to sentimentalise or cheapen the love of God, which puts all our existence into crisis, the ethical best of it as well as the ethical worst. But if we are incarnational Christians, we flesh out the judgement of God not by being judgemental, but by bearing in our own lives the cross; by destroying the platitudes of our self-righteousness, and by suffering the moral ambiguity and complexity of the actual world. To withdraw to the apparent safety of ethical blacks and whites, to tell others what to do without sharing the insideness of their predicament, is to retreat from the generosity of the Christian Gospel, and the flexibility of grace.

Response to Nigel M de S Cameron

Dr Cameron's paper clearly invites detailed and sustained discussion, well beyond the scope of this reply. What follows merely indicates the direction such conversation might follow.

I appreciate his desire to go beyond the superficial absence of formal Scripture discussions or mere 'text-slinging'. I share also his basic sense that we are all made to be persons in the image of God, and that the continuity from conception through birth can be broken only by convention (although some conventions are more intelligible than others).

A Historical and exegetical

(1) Dr Cameron makes much of the axiomatic rejection of abortion in the Jewish and Old Testament background to Christian debate. It has been pointed out elsewhere, however, that tradition was far more diverse than Professor Metzger allows. The study by A Unterman, *Jews, their religious beliefs and practices*,[1] documents extensive disagreement within Orthodox and Hasidic Judaism. This includes arguments from Scripture and tradition about risk to the mother's life, to her psychic health, risks of deformity in the child, and a variety of social grounds. It specifically mentions that termination of pregnancy up to 40 days was excluded from the prohibition on killing. The 'taken for granted' ethics alleged by Professor Metzger disappear.

(2) There is a need to relate Scripture's treatment of ethical issues to the social context in which they emerged. Dr Cameron fails to do so, for instance in his brief discussion of 'the widely recognised exceptional reasons of judicial execution and just warfare'.

I am unclear as to how Dr Cameron decides whether *any* ethical practice implied or alluded to in Scripture is actually determined by theology or by sociological or cultural factors. In fact, can these ever be confidently isolated? Should we not, rather, modify these claims to offer '*the* biblical perspective', to offers of '*a* biblical perspective' or even of 'a perspective on the Bible'?

B Doctrinal and Theological

While human persons are celebrated in Scripture and early Christian theology as bearers of the image of God, it is surely not as 'members of the species'. The *imago Dei* is historical rather, and eschatological, to do with the community of creation whose identity is defined by God and his future in freedom and love. Certainly this image of God does not depend on discriminatory qualities, like intelligence, colour or health, for example. But nor is it an automatic consequence of our biology or genetics. It belongs to the dynamic relating of God to us. This of course in no way strengthens a 'soft line' on abortion, but it may undercut the 'biological pride' of which there are whiffs in Dr Cameron's doctrine of creation. The Old Testament more realistically confirms that as biological beings, we are dust, the stuff of the cosmos.

(3) While sharing Dr Cameron's conviction that the incarnation hallows the human person and all creation, I think traditional Christology is a far more double-edged weapon in the abortion debate than he acknowledges. It is not, despite classical orthodoxy, 'man's bearing the divine image' which makes incarnation possible. Rather the reverse: it is the Incarnate Christ who creates and sustains our divine image. Christology is the preamble to creation.

Furthermore, the biblical passages about the conception, ante-natal life and virgin birth of Jesus generate *more* problems surely within the abortion debate, the *more* seriously one takes them as furnishing literal biological information. For if the embryo emerging from Mary's Fallopian tubes was fertilised without male human sperm, its biological and genetic constitution is so *unlike* ours that its ethical relevance to ordinary humanness is questionable. If, on the other hand, God provided the male, human sperm, this is paganism. Dr Cameron ignores the vast field of debate within Christian theology about the origins, intentions and subsequent theological use of the birth narratives in the early Church.

C Ethical and Pastoral

(4) Dietrich Bonhoeffer begins his *Ethics* with the haunting sentences:

> The knowledge of good and evil seems to be the aim of all ethical reflections.
> The first task of Christian ethics is to invalidate this knowledge.

He then enlarges on the profound ambivalences of ethics, precisely in the light of an incarnate God who does not destroy but embraces our broken, muddy, ragged, sinful world. My feeling is that Dr Cameron profoundly distrusts such an implication of incarnation, being confident of his rescue from uncertainty and error. This seems to me a crucial core of difference between two theologies, one suggesting that faith simplifies the ethical world, the other suggesting that you explore a hallowed world by suffering its full, dark complexity as your own.

(5) I find it pastorally unedifying that Dr Cameron does scant justice to his opponents in the debate. The rhetoric and innuendo of his paper constantly imputes trivial motives (and feeble intellect) to those involved in deciding on abortion or theologians defending such decisions. This cheapens an earnest and passionate discussion.

Undoubtedly there is a pole of human carelessness, individual and corporate, where life is so devalued and unhallowed that human beings, embryonic or mature, are killed, one way or another, without thought or attention. I am not convinced that our present legislation or medical practice about abortion embodies or supports such carelessness (although much else about our national life does).

Rather, the shift marked by David Steel's bill seems to me to have emerged from a pastoral concern which I find largely absent, or at least not realistically charted, in Dr Cameron's comments on raped women, bearers of grossly-deformed fetuses, teenage/student/single parents and the like. It is not to *punish* a spina bifida baby for its imperfections, but to save it from a probably short and entirely painful life that parents and doctors may decide to abort. No doubt it is a world far enough from the Kingdom of God which fails to cherish and nurture its present 'unwanted children' along with other weak, marginal or deviant groups. But until domestic, national or international resources are transformed in order to care for them, it is intolerable that every raped woman, every child whose sexual experiments end in pregnancy, every family facing the strain of absorbing major deformity, should be scapegoats for our moral self-righteousness.

The levels and densities of pain, fear, despair, anxiety, self-hatred and loving concern involved in decisions about abortion are barely recognised and certainly not penetrated by Dr Cameron's ethical absolutes. And the lifegiving kindness of God seems to be more manifest in a less aloof response to the integrity and passion of those who face the abortion dilemma with different responses.

Note to Response

1   A Unterman, *Jews, their religious beliefs and practices* (Routledge and Kegan Paul, 1981).

Response to Elizabeth Templeton

I am grateful for the opportunity to respond briefly to Elizabeth Templeton's chapter, and regret that the necessary brevity of these remarks makes it impossible to treat more adequately (and perhaps more fairly) her wide-ranging arguments.

(1) The fact that Mrs Templeton manages to write her chapter on what the Bible says on this subject while referring to it hardly at all is interesting in itself. But it will not do to suggest — as she does — that the kind of case I have outlined against abortion is a natural consequence of expecting the Bible to give what she calls 'blow-by-blow directions from God'. The irony is that some of the Christians who *do* expect it to be 'a blueprint of immediate divine directives about contemporary dilemmas' are actually in favour of abortion, on the ground that nowhere does the Bible condemn it in so many words! (This is the position of R F R Gardner in his influential book, *Abortion: The Personal Dilemma.*)

On the contrary, my central argument is not that the Bible answers the question, 'Is abortion right?', but that it answers the prior question, 'Is the child not yet born a human being made in the image of God?' This is an altogether more sophisticated approach to biblical interpretation, and it has led Professor T F Torrance to declare that 'the Abortion Act opened up a legal way for the horrifying slaughter of many thousands of helpless babies, which must surely be the greatest moral blot on the British parliament and people this century'.[1] Perhaps I can quote him again.

> 'Since,' he writes, 'in his Incarnation ... the Lord Jesus assumed our human nature, gathering up all its stages and healing them in his own human life, *including conception*, he thereby gave the human embryo an inviolable status from the very beginning of his or her creaturely existence.'[2]

It is impossible to dismiss such an argument as depending upon a naïve approach to biblical interpretation, since it rests rather on the fundamental doctrine of the incarnation and its implications for our understanding of the nature of human existence.

(2) Mrs Templeton seems prepared to admit much of the case that is usually advanced against abortion, while herself subscribing to thoroughly liberal practical criteria for when it is permissible. She regards abortion as a serious matter (p 22).

> There is of course something of vital importance indicated by the language of 'rights' of the fetus — namely that what is a potential person cannot be discarded like a piece of litter.

33

B

Elsewhere she can refer to the 'planned destruction of a person, or a potential person'. She had deliberately 'not argued the permissive case in terms of reducing the status of the fetus'. So candid an admission leaves her with a task which seems, and in the event proves, impossible. The kind of liberal abortion she advocates can never be made to square with any serious assessment of the nature of the fetus. Her seemingly unequivocal support for the present Abortion Act (which is 'responsible ... and should be supported and strengthened by Christians ... rather than ... attacked'), and her support for abortion even as a means of population control, put her, as a simple matter of fact, well outside the middle ground of responsible Christian moral opinion.

(3) Mrs Templeton presents her case in the form of a series of theses. The first three are directed at one conventional Roman Catholic way of arguing against abortion as, in effect, an extension of artificial contraception. For present purposes I am prepared to accept the general thrust of her arguments, since they do not interact at all with most Protestant discussion.

The crux of her argument, however, would seem to lie in the contention that 'there is no absolute theological basis for the assertion that life is, at all costs, to be saved'; and to this we now turn. There are two sides to her case. First, is it right to let 'a child be born in a situation where its life is likely to be, or to cause, an overwhelming experience of negativity within the world it will concretely inhabit'?

Well, if only it were so simple. The campaigners for abortion argued long and hard that it would do away with child abuse, which has of course tragically spread by leaps and bounds since 1967; and the irony is that what little evidence we have suggests that children abused by their parents are more likely to have been 'wanted' than 'unwanted'.

We certainly have no way of determining which babies will be happy when they grow up and which will not, and if what Mrs Templeton is proposing is the ideal of a Utilitarian calculus of joy and sadness which must result in, say, a score of seven out of ten before an infant who is conceived is allowed to be born, she is radically departing from the Christian tradition. *Even with certain knowledge* it would be profoundly undesirable to subject new human lives to such an exercise in quality control. But, as it is, we have no way of judging who will be happy and who will not. The affluent and healthy may end up miserable, and the poor and handicapped happy. And in any event, what about 'quality control' in parallel situations later in life? What of the road accident victim, the multiple sclerosis sufferer or the persistent depressive who can expect only a life which is 'likely to be, or to cause, an overwhelming experience of negativity within the world [they] will concretely inhabit'?

Mrs Templeton makes much of the very difficult situations in life when people are faced with the question of whether to continue with a pregnancy.

The trouble is that an abortion climate makes it more difficult to deal with certain problems and easier to respond to others: living as we do in an abortion climate, we are beguiled into the belief that abortion is a little thing and these others, the problems of handicap, the difficulty of extreme social or personal circumstances, are greater things. These experiences of negativity, of hurt and pain, are themselves relative. The *supremely* negative fact is the fact that, in abortion, for whatever reason, we kill our babies.

Second, the other side of Mrs Templeton's argument turns on the fact that Christians are generally prepared to take human life in other contexts. This brings us to the knub of the issue. If there are such contexts, *on what ground do we approve the taking of life? Are those grounds appropriate here?* Mrs Templeton does not say whether she approves of the Church's support of, or acquiescence in, the taking of human life apart from abortion. One might be forgiven for supposing that she may not, in which case this entire line of argument would be merely *ad hominem* and her ideal would be that of a Church which denounced the taking of life in every context other than that of abortion. But such a supposition may be unfair. Mrs Templeton may actually support the historic Christian defence of (some) warfare and, indeed, the death penalty.

In any event, the question we must ask is what grounds have been advanced to justify the taking of human life? The morality of 'just' warfare and the capital sentence is the morality of human life in the balance — when one life is in direct conflict with another. It has an analogy with the case of abortion in only one instance, and that when the mother's life is under threat.

Mrs Templeton may think otherwise, but we need to be prepared for the consequences of accepting the principle that human life can be taken for lesser reasons. In his valuable booklet *The Christian and the Unborn Child,*[3] Oliver O'Donovan, an Anglican who is Regius Professor of Moral and Pastoral Theology at Oxford, puts this well in a simple illustration. Because we live in a fallen world, as Mrs Templeton heavily underlines and as we can scarcely deny, the birth of a child like many other events can have tragic consequences. Sometimes (although not usually) they may be foreseen. The question remains whether our kindness towards child, mother or society at large should ever lead us to kill.

Professor O'Donovan writes as follows:

Let us imagine a daughter caring for a difficult, but not senile, mother, in an area where neither Social Services nor neighbours were available to help her bear the load. The doctor judges that the daughter is heading for a major, and permanent, breakdown, and sees no way of avoiding it short of killing the mother. If we valued mental health equivalently to human life we might feel able to advise him to take that drastic step (provided he could get away with it). This is a conclusion from which most of us would shrink. In the last resort it is hard to accept that mental health or physical health or any *social* good is a value quite equivalent to human life.[3]

Notes to Response

1 *Test-Tube Babies: Morals — Science — and the Law* (Edinburgh, 1984), p 6.
2 ibid, p 10.
3 *The Christian and the Unborn Child* (Nottingham, 1973), p 19.

3

The Fetus as a Person

Is the fetus a person? The first thing to be said about this question is that it is a great improvement on many of the questions which are asked in the context of the debate on abortion. The question which is often asked is: 'When does life begin?' — which is something of a non-question, because it is quite obvious that anything present from the moment of fertilisation is alive. Whatever else the early embryo is or is not, it is unquestionably a living organism engaged in a process of growth and development. Of course, sperm and eggs before fertilisation are also living organisms, but without the potential, on their own, for growth and development; the life contained within the embryo is thus of a significantly different order than that which is evident in the sperm or egg. Nor is the question, 'When does *human* life begin?' much of an improvement. For there is no doubt that life at this very early stage is human life. It makes no sense to think of it as some neutral, anonymous, unnamed sort of life. It is not plant life (*eg* the life of a honeysuckle), nor animal life (*eg* the life of a hedgehog), but human life. The fact that it has been conceived of human parents is enough to tell us that.

The question, 'Is the fetus a person?', is more helpful. Indeed, it is probably the question which those who ask the above-cited non-questions are really getting at. But it is still perhaps not *the* most helpful question to ask, because it prompts in turn a not easily resolved question: 'How should we define a person?' In a recent book on abortion I came across the following definition:

> A person is in a strict sense a being who possesses the developed capacity to engage in acts of *intellect* (to think, use language, *etc*), acts of emotion (to love, hate, *etc*), and acts of *will* (to make moral choices, to affirm spiritual ideals, *etc*).[1]

What is described here is an individual with a developed capacity for rational, moral and spiritual agency. Clearly these are important capacities which appear to mark human beings out from the rest of the animal creation. When individuals make use of these capacities in a positive and creative way we may be inclined to say that they are realising their potential as persons. But it is striking how often this potential goes unrealised. In some cases, the capacity is present in an individual but is not developed, *eg*, where someone fails to sharpen his intellect through lack of stimulating company and educational opportunity, or where he becomes conditioned by his peer-group in his attitude to moral issues and so fails to make meaningful choices. In other cases, the individual has been born with a severe mental handicap which means that his or her potential to develop these capacities is greatly reduced, however helpful an environment is provided. Then there are individuals who suffer serious brain damage in an accident, or contract senile dementia, and lose the developed capacities which they once had. Finally, babies who are born healthy and who may reasonably be expected to develop these capacities in the future cannot be said to be rational, moral and spiritual agents in the early years of life. There are thus several categories of person who do not possess the developed capacity described, but we would still hesitate to withdraw the title 'person' from any of them. There is tragedy when human beings fail to realise their potential, or lose the abilities they once had, but this happens to all of us to some extent. 'Persons' we remain, despite this falling short of an ideal.

It thus seems that if we are to include the notorious under-achiever, the child with Down's Syndrome, the comatose victim of a road accident and the newly born baby as persons along with most of our fellow-humans, we need a less strict definition of person than that which was cited above. We would have to place far less emphasis on capacities. We might well be left with a fairly minimalist description which might amount to little more than 'a living member of the human species'. Nevertheless, we can see what the question, 'Is the fetus a person?', is getting at. What is fundamentally at stake is whether the fetus commands a *status* and deserves a *respect* comparable to that accorded to human persons outside the womb. In short, is such status linked to attainment of a particular stage in the developmental process? Developmental process is not usually linked to sanctity of life outside the womb. To kill a baby just two hours old is as much murder as to kill a sportsman at the height of his power or a bank manager who has recently retired. It is true that with regard to the severely handicapped, comatose or demented, many would question whether every effort should necessarily be made to *save* life (*eg* in circumstances where they contracted a serious illness on top of their existing complaint), but few would say that we should actively *take* it. Their standing as persons still provides them with protection. With regard to the fetus, however, the situation is radically different. Fetal lives are regularly taken in the act of abortion. The lack of developmental attainment of the fetus gives it a much reduced status in the eyes of those who sanction a liberal approach to abortion. As Christians, what ought our attitude to be?

First of all, I believe that we should attend closely to the witness of biblical writers and the Christian tradition. Others in this volume have written much more fully on this subject, so I will say little, but a summary of my conclusions is appropriate. There are several biblical passages which suggest a high view of life in the womb. Human fetuses are seen as objects of God's creative activity, loving care and special calling (see, for example, Ps. 139:13–16, Job 10:8–12, Isa. 49:1, Jer. 1:5, Luke 1:15, 44). The silence of the biblical writers on the actual subject of abortion (a phenomenon common among neighbour-ing peoples in biblical times) is more satisfactorily explained by the likelihood that they regarded the practice as unthinkable, rather than that they viewed it as tolerable. On the other hand, there is one passage (Exod. 21:22–25) which, if translated and interpreted in a certain way, appears to rank the life of a pregnant mother more highly than that of a fetus.[2] The ambiguity introduced by this passage into the biblical witness helps to account for the existence of different strands of opinion in the Church's tradition. One strand of opinion has insisted on the full personal status of the fetus from the time of conception. The other strand, drawing on the Septuagint translation of Exodus 21:22–25 as well as Platonic ideas about the nature of the soul, has argued that the fetus is not animated by a soul until some way into pregnancy (around 40 days at least in the case of a male). While modern theologians are less happy about using terminology of the soul, there are representatives of this view who identify the emergence of a subject of consciousness (linked to fetal brain development) as a similar key point of discontinuity.[3] However, it is noteworthy that up until very recent times both strands of opinion were united in believing that abortion was wrong. Those who took the second view simply regarded abortions which took place before animation of the soul as warranting less serious punishment than those which took place after that stage. Despite the differences of opinion about the precise status of the fetus at varying stages of development, there was fundamental agreement that the life of the fetus was sacred and deserved respect.

Nevertheless, we do not feel bound by the verdict of past generations of Christians. Until the present century Christian opinion was united in its abhorrence of artificial methods of birth control, but now the majority of Christians (including many in the Roman Catholic Church) accept that there is a legitimate place for them. The change of opinion on this issue has, no doubt, been partly a matter of responding to and following secular trends; but it has been justified in terms of a fresh analysis of the act of sexual intercourse.[4] The relational, as distinct from procreative, aspect of sexual intercourse has given much more emphasis, and since the natural processes dictate that many acts of intercourse contain no procreative potential, but still remain valid as expressions of a loving relationship, deliberate pursuit of the latter end alone may sometimes be valid. In the case of abortion, the more liberal approach adopted by many Christians is also a matter of responding to and following secular trends, but it might too be the result of a fresh analysis of the issue. Could there be something about the significance of fetal life which Christians of past ages have missed, something which makes resorting to abortion easier to justify?

Certainly much more is now known about the development of the fetus. We now know that from the moment when the male sperm fertilises the female egg, the resulting embryo is equipped with a particular genetic package which determines all sorts of details about the person in later life, *eg* identity of sex, colour of eyes, colour of hair. Within two weeks the embryo, barring a miscarriage, will have implanted in the woman's womb. After three weeks, activity of the heart begins. After five weeks there are reflex movements in the spinal cord. After six and a half weeks (about the time abortions begin to be done), fingers and toes have formed and major organs such as heart, lungs, gut and kidneys are all there in rudimentary form. The brain has already developed to a size where it swamps everything else. Between eight and 12 weeks the fetus doubles in length, grows finger-nails, starts sucking its thumb, develops sexual organs and — in many cases — is capable of registering brain-waves (this is the peak period for performing abortions; from eight weeks the term 'fetus' replaces that of 'embryo'). Between 18 and 20 weeks, or thereabouts, the mother starts to feel the child moving, the experience known as 'quickening'. By 24 weeks the child may, with the help of the most advanced equipment be able to survive outside the womb ('viability').

About the biological facts there is little disagreement; but what significance to read into these different stages arouses much disagreement. Some people (Christians probably not being very prominent among them) would say that none of these stages warrant according the fetus the status of a person. The obvious stage for according personal status is birth, because then the child becomes independent of its mother; it is no longer physically connected to its mother's body. Clearly birth is of great psychological significance both to the child and its parents, but it is doubtful whether this startling change in location establishes the ground for a comparable shift in status. The child differs little in its capacities immediately after birth from the child immediately before; and although the direct link is severed, the baby will still be hopelessly dependent on a mother or some human substitute for a mother for a long time to come.

There is certainly a growing band of opinion (with Christians quite prominent in this group) which argues that a particular stage in brain development is the crucial moment. This may be on the grounds that brain function is related to sentience, and if the fetus was to feel pain in the act of being aborted, then something immoral would be done to it, but not otherwise. Or it may be on the grounds that the brain is vital for those activities like thinking, deciding and communicating which we regard as hallmarks of personal existence. Christian theologians have often located the image of God in human capacities such as these; it is therefore plausible to suggest that God does not stamp his particular image on man until the point when the embryonic brain shows the first vestiges of activity. Moreover, an analogy is drawn between our criteria for determining when a person has ceased to exist (which is an irreparable cessation of brain function) and the criteria we should use for determining when a person is starting to exist (when the brain does start to function).

Fashionable though this stress on brain function is, the position is chock-full with problems. By itself sentience is a quite unsatisfactory criterion, otherwise it would be perfectly acceptable to kill innocent people as long as one could do so painlessly. While the brain is obviously a *sine qua non* of human existence in a way that the thumb, for instance, is not, it is a reductionist interpretation of the *imago Dei* concept which sees it only in terms of activities performed by the brain. It is equally plausible to argue that if we take the word 'image' seriously, it must mean that human beings reflect God; and a reflection takes in the entirety of one's being. Why then should we not believe that there is already a faint reflection, that God has already started on his work of creating a replica, right at the earliest beginnings of embryonic life? The advocates of brain function as crucial for ascribing personhood actually seem caught between resting their case on something that has actually happened and something that will potentially happen. For what excites such people about the 40 day old embryo whose brain is flickering into consciousness is the *potential* which it now has for becoming a rational, morally responsible and spiritually aware human being. It is still very far from being that at 40 days! If they waited for the potential to be anything like realised, they would have to wait at the earliest until the child went to nursery school, and at the latest until well into adulthood! But if their case depends to such a large extent on the notion of the brain's potential, why do they not respect the potential for all the future brain development which is already contained within the embryo from the outset? Again, this potential for future development clearly distinguishes the embryo from the person whose brain has ceased to function. If someone who was in a coma had a prospect of resuming normal brain functioning, we would respect his or her right to live. Why treat the embryo differently?

Another important consideration is this. Advocates of brain development are actually not in full agreement as to which point in brain development is the crucial one. Measurement of embryonic brain activity by electroencephalogram (EEG) reveals no consistent pattern, so that one embryo might record brain waves at eight weeks, another not until 12. Ought then the right to live depend on speed of development, or the sensitivity of measuring equipment? However, if one was to adopt the oft-recommended approach and err on the side of caution, so that one treats all human fetuses by the yardstick of the fastest developer, then one would still have to conclude that the great majority of abortions currently practised involve the killing of persons (given that the peak period for abortions is between eight and 12 weeks, with many more being done thereafter).

Perhaps because this is an unpalatable conclusion, perhaps because neither brain development nor birth (and certainly not stages in between, like quickening and viability) can bear the weight put on them as 'decisive moments', some people opt for the solution that, somewhere between the two the fetus *gradually* assumes the status and rights of a person. Therefore, later abortions are harder to justify than earlier ones; the reasons required to justify them are proportionately more grave; but there is no point in fetal life at which we can definitely say that we are killing a person, nor that the possibility of abortion should be definitely ruled out (other than for purely medical reasons).

This idea that our respect for fetuses should gradually increase certainly ties in with the way most expectant parents gradually come to regard the fetus as more precious the longer a pregnancy lasts. But that understandable psychological trait is hardly sufficient ground for making a moral judgement with life-or-death implications. Something more objective is needed, which the gradualist way of looking at things fails to provide. Indeed, it is difficult to see why, along this line of approach, the gradual process of becoming a person should necessarily be seen as complete by the point of birth. In view of the high state of dependence and limited intellectual and physical capacities of a baby or infant, why not postpone the ascription of *full* personhood until some time after birth? Of course, one would give it a higher degree of protection than one would ascribe to a fetus, but the possibility of killing it in sufficiently grave circumstances should not be ruled out. However, very few gradualists follow their argument to its logical conclusion. Somewhere along the line they write a decisive moment (usually birth) into the gradual process. The gradualist viewpoint is probably more common among secular thinkers than Christian ones, but the latter category appears to be growing. It seems to me a viewpoint quite devoid of theological pedigree. The notion of human creatures slowly, imperceptibly becoming person (*ie* earning, by dint of gradually increased capacities, the right to be regarded as worthy of protection and respect) is utterly foreign to the biblical picture of a God who sees dignity in people where other people can see none, and in the process of seeing dignity *confers* dignity upon them.[5]

In view of the unsatisfactory nature of the alternatives, I am driven to the conclusion that to choose any point other than fertilisation for ascribing personal status to the embryo is highly arbitrary. In other words, fresh analysis of the data relating to fetuses drives me back to one of the two mainstream Christian positions regarding the status of the fetus. There are of course arguments regularly lodged against this position. For instance, a great many fertilised eggs miscarry at an early stage, sometimes even before a woman knows that she is pregnant. Can these really be persons who have perished? The answer 'yes' is not as silly as it may sound at first. The history of the world is full of infants who have perished early, at birth or soon after, and their personal status goes unquestioned; the phenomenon of miscarriage simply shows a similar sort of occurrence happening even earlier. The fact that cell division to produce twinning may occur up to 14 days after fertilisation is used as an argument against stress on the embryo's genetic uniqueness from the point of fusion. Yet a cell destined to 'twin' retains its genetic *particularity*; that particularity may well determine the fact that it will split; and perhaps the best way to describe it at its earliest stage is as two persons under the *appearance* of being one. Another argument is that parents do not usually *feel* a great loss when a miscarriage happens early; as I have already said, the embryo or fetus is felt to be more of a person the longer it survives. But again, we need to be extremely careful what conclusions we draw from people's feelings. The mother of an eight week old fetus who wants an abortion is likely to feel that it is less of a person than does the mother of an eight week old fetus who wants a baby. But if the first girl was to see her fetus on scan, her feelings might well change — which often happens. Yet the extent of the development of the fetus would not have significantly changed before and after the scan — simply her attitude towards it.

The objections to regarding the early embryo as a person, therefore, seem to me less substantial than the problems connected with any other viewpoint. They are problems which have more to do with our limited powers of imagination, our reluctance to extend our concept of what constitutes a person, than with the actual biological data. I would certainly grant that dogmatism is out of order here. We cannot know for certain that God sees early embryos as just as much persons, as equally precious, as joint inheritors of eternity, as he does those who are grown-up members of the human race. But in view of his persistent concern for the outcast, his choice of a little nation, his habit of turning human values and hierarchies on their head, I submit that it would be entirely in keeping with his character if he does. And analysis of the biological data leads one to marvel at the awesome potential that is already contained within the embryo from conception, rather than to be struck by some decisive moment of discontinuity at a later stage in the process.

Of course, if one's imagination does baulk at the notion of a miniscule embryo as a person, this need not necessarily lead one to a position where one accords the embryo no respect or rights at all. If one only regards the embryo (or the fetus) as a potential person, then that potential is surely worth taking seriously. A young child who is *potentially* a sexually active adult, or a politically active citizen, surely has the right to have his genitalia or franchise retained intact until the moment when he can *actually* use them. If castration or a tyrannical take-over represent major injustices to someone not yet actively involved in sexual or political processes, abortion can be said to represent a major injustice inflicted on someone who is not yet enjoying life in a very active sense. Alternatively, if one takes a more agnostic position, and says 'the fetus may be a person, but I'm not sure', it makes sense to give to this possibly personal creature the benefit of the doubt. It is irresponsible to use uncertainty as a cloak for excusing an action so momentous as the extermination of human life. There is therefore no logical reason why opposition to abortion need be confined to those who are *convinced* that the fetus is a person, although it is understandable that the stronger the conviction is, the more committed the opposition is likely to be.

However, it is now time to examine, and in the process to qualify, an assumption which has been apparently implicit throughout my argument: *viz*, it is wrong to kill human persons. Although this certainly holds good as a general rule, few except extreme pacifists have believed that it is *invariably* wrong to take the life of a fellow-person. And if killing can be justified in certain exceptional cases, might not abortion constitute such an exception?

If one looks at the Old Testament, the taking of human life is certainly seen as justified in two sorts of situations: a divinely approved war, and as a capital punishment for serious offences. This killing appears to be justified on two main grounds: (a) an act of judgement on guilty parties — a notion which to some extent applies to war as well as capital punishment; and (b) a means of preventing calamitous events, *eg* lawbreakers running amok in society, or the destruction of God's chosen people. Following this Old Testament line of thought, and even when one has taken into account the stronger emphasis on values like peace and mercy in the New Testament, many Christians have felt that the taking of life is justified in wars which may be deemed 'just', and/or capital punishment for an offence such as murder.

There is, to be sure, an alternative Christian view, which objects in a more wholesale way to the taking of human life, which sees the New Testament more in terms of superseding the Old Testament, and which regards sayings of Jesus like 'turn the other cheek', 'love your enemy' and 'take up your cross' as incompatible with killing a fellow-person. Christians who take this view are pacifists, opposed to capital punishment and, assuming they regard fetuses as persons, and also that they are consistent (which Christians, just like other people, not always are!), they will be anti-abortionist in attitude as well.

Personally, I believe that there can be such a thing as a — relatively — just war, and that capital punishment is a defensible option within the context of some societies, so I am at least prepared to concede the possibility that the taking of human life can be justified. I would regard the killing carried out in a just war as essentially a killing of guilty parties, and (in line with the traditional just war criteria) would oppose any direct assaults on the lives of innocent bystanders in war.

However, there are some exceptional situations in which Christians of both just war and pacifist schools of thought would probably agree that the killing of innocent people may be justified. The two types of example which spring to mind are: (a) putting a dying person out of his misery when there is no medical aid available, *eg* a mortally wounded soldier in terrible agony; and (b) the unintended killing of person B as the result of concentrating all available resources on saving person A, where it is impossible to save both persons. An example of this in the context of abortion is where a cancerous womb threatens the lives of both a pregnant mother and her fetus. If nothing is done both will die; but if the womb is removed the mother will survive, although the fetus will inevitably perish. Even Roman Catholics with their strict anti-abortionist stance would agree to hysterectomy in such an instance, regarding this as a case of indirect abortion and justifying the action by use of the principle of double effect.[6]

I shall now briefly consider three other categories of 'hard cases' where abortions may be requested, seeking to be consistent in applying the criteria for the taking of life outlined above. First, there are cases where the fetus has been diagnosed — certainly in some cases, probably in others — as carrying a serious handicap. In these circumstances abortion is often defended either on the grounds that it is saving the person who would develop, from a great deal of suffering and misery in later life, or because it is saving the parent(s) from the immense burden of looking after a seriously handicapped person. However, neither of these considerations would be deemed sufficient to justify killing a seriously handicapped person after birth. We do not approve euthanasia (mercy-killing), and we regard the proper response to the suffering of either a handicapped person or his parents as being relief of the suffering, improvement of facilities for handicapped people, sharing the burden of care for them, and so on. We respect the handicapped person's basic right to live, believing (rightly) that it is presumptuous to say of someone else that the quality of his or her life is such that it is not worth living. If we take the view that the handicapped fetus is just as much a person as the handicapped child or adult, then our attitude should be the same: one of respect for life, and concern to provide the best possible resources for the care of the handicapped.

I grant that there may be a few cases where the diagnosed handicap is so extreme, and the knowledge gleaned through diagnosis sufficiently certain, that abortion would be justified. I have in mind cases like the anencephalic of whom one can be confident that he or she will not survive birth. The Church of Scotland Board of Social Responsibility Study Group on Abortion Report refers to this type of case when it says that, 'There are conditions which are incompatible with life after birth and abortion merely brings forward the inevitable to shorten the parents' period of distress while the mother carries the baby'. In such a case, aborting the anencephalic fetus is perhaps comparable to hastening the end of the dying soldier. It is more a case of relieving the misery of the mother carrying the fetus than relieving the misery of the fetus itself, but the important point of comparison is that it is mercifully bringing forward the conclusion of a definitely doomed life.

What can be said with confidence about the handicapped fetus is that it is an innocent party, and innocent parties do not deserve to die. The position of the fetus conceived as a result of rape, another oft-cited hard case, is a little more complicated. There is a possible ground for arguing that abortion in the case of rape may be justified if one takes a just-war type of position towards the taking of human life. Let us consider comparable features between the two situations. When one takes up arms to defend a just cause against a guilty agressor — an opponent whom in one's own judgement is fighting an *unjust* war — the people with whom one does battle are not necessarily the most directly guilty parties themselves, (no Allied soldier was able to get a crack at Hitler!), but *representatives* of the guilty party. Enemy soldiers may of course fully concur with the unjust cause for which they are fighting, in which case they participate in the guilt of the instigator of the war. But they may have been unwillingly dragooned into fighting; nevertheless, they remain representatives of the guilty party, and killing them in defence of one's just cause is probably justified. It would be preferable if one had the opportunity to discover first whether they supported the unjust cause or not, but the fact is that one does not have such an opportunity!

In a way the embryo conceived as the result of rape is the representative of a guilty party. It is a hostile intruder, even though it has been unwillingly dragooned into the part. Although not consenting to the act of aggression, its expulsion might be justified, like that of the unhappy soldier, on the grounds of self-defence. The rapist alone is responsible for the existence of the child; why should his victim be saddled with the obligation to bring *his* child into the world?

Although all my compassionate instincts make me want to agree with abortion in this situation, I have to admit that the analogy with war does not hold good entirely. For the conscripted soldier is a genuine threat to *life*, whereas the embryo growing within the raped woman is unlikely to constitute that. Certainly it threatens the mother's peace of mind, continued well-being, and her desire to banish the humiliating experience of rape to the back of her mind. It is even conceivable that a pregnancy resulting from rape can appear so devastating that it poses an indirect threat to life, *eg* by making the mother strongly suicidal. But in most circumstances one's impression is that the threat posed by pregnancy after rape, although serious, is not quite tantamount to a threat to life.

Abortion therefore *might* be defended from a just war position, but the analogy is not wholly convincing. From a pacifist position, abortion in the case of rape could not be justified. For the pacifist view is that one should never respond to violence with lethal violence; one never takes human life into one's own hands, however great the level of provocation.

An interesting aspect of the rape dilemma is that where a mother does decide to have the child, we regard such behaviour as heroic. In that case, it seems illogical to regard the opposite course of action as justified and within the mother's rights. Nevertheless, the fact that we combine these two attitudes is explicable. Of some self-sacrificial actions it may be said that, noble as they are, it would be unreasonable to *demand* that other people perform them. I would therefore be unhappy with a law which actually prohibited abortion after rape; on the other hand, allowing abortion on this ground alone (danger to life apart) would be extremely problematical, because proving that rape has taken place can be difficult to establish. Genuine rape victims might not have the issue settled until far into the pregnancy, which would make the prospect of an abortion more dangerous; and bogus rape victims would probably use the ground as a legal loophole.

Finally I turn to cases where both partners have fully consented to the sexual act, but pregnancy was not intended. The termination of the pregnancy is desired because the advent of a child will bring considerable inconvenience and cause a major change of plan on the part of the mother (and, if he stays with her, the father). Abortion will almost certainly be requested and quite likely be granted on the grounds of threat to health. But although unwanted pregnancy undoubtedly brings strain — a strain which might in some cases, but not in others, be construed as a threat to health — this cannot be a satisfactory justification for abortion. The threat to the health of the mother or other members of her family should not weigh as highly as the threat which abortion poses to the life of the fetus. On any normal scale of values life ranks more highly than health, because without life there can be no values. Unfortunately, the widespread current tendency to regard the fetus as less than a person, or nearly a person, or not yet a person, obscures this very simple moral truth. If we do regard human fetuses as persons, then we are forced to conclude that the overwhelming majority of abortions which have been practised in the United Kingdom since the 1967 Abortion Act are morally indefensible.

Notes to Paper 3

1   Robert N Wennberg, *Life in the Balance: Exploring the Abortion Controversy* (Eerdmans, Grand Rapids, Michigan, 1985), p 33.

2   However, the sense is altered radically by whether a miscarriage is referred to (see RSV translation) or a premature birth (see NIV).

3   See, for example, the majority view on the Church of England Board for Social Responsibility Working Party on Human Fertilisation and Embryology, expressed in their Report, *Person Origins* (CIO, 1985), pp 28–34.

4   As found, for instance, in the Church of England Report, *The Family in Contemporary Society* (SPCK, 1958).

5   This seems to me the picture presented by the attitude of the father to the son in the Parable of the Prodigal Son, for instance.

6   This principle may be summed up thus: 'One is justified in permitting incidental evil effects from one's good actions if there is a proportionate reason'. I have discussed the principle of double effect in my *Key Themes in Roman Catholic Ethics: Nature, Character and Rules* (Grove Booklet on Ethics, No 60, Nottingham, 1986).

4

The Moral Significance of the Embryo and the Fetus

Introduction

When I originally agreed to write this contribution, I agreed also to the editor's general description that it would be 'a paper arguing for the increasing recognition of rights in the fetus as it develops'. Since I believe that something of this kind can be argued for, I have tried to do this in the second section of what follows. As I thought about this contribution, however, it became increasingly clear to me that the most crucial moral and theological arguments about abortion have less to do with abortion as such than with how we think about God. In a recent debate on abortion, indeed, it became all too painfully obvious that the sincere Christian with whom I was arguing thought so differently to me about God's ways with us, that agreement on the moral issues seemed infinitely far away. Yet we recited the same creed, addressed Our Father in the same words. Perhaps there is nothing new in this. 'Both read the Bible day and night, but thou read'st black where I read white,' as Blake put it. It is nevertheless a great difficulty, which makes it necessary before writing specifically about abortion and fetal life, to indicate the general theological and moral context in which the subject is to be discussed. I would like to begin, however, with another personal anecdote.

1 General Theological and Moral Considerations

Spiders
One summer evening when I was a small boy, I squashed a large spider on my bedroom floor. I still remember the horror with which I then saw numbers of tiny spiders emerging from it. Panicking, I tried to kill them too. That was a long time ago and of a different order of magnitude to the human death which may be involved in an abortion. But I want to begin with this recollection because some of the issues it raises are not unrelated to that.

Some people, of course, might argue that my encounter with the spider raised no significant moral issues. That, as far as I remember, was more or less my own initial response to the experience. I came to terms with it by deciding that they were, after all, 'only spiders', and by reflecting that my

49

friends who lived on farms would have been pretty scornful of any further scruples. Looking back on that response now, I suppose I would have to agree that my motives were hardly of the best. It would, as it happened, have been an easy enough matter to transfer the spider gently to the sturdy clematis growing outside my bedroom window. Or again, I could have left it where it was, and with any luck discovered how spiders are born. In killing it therefore, I may have lost an opportunity of having my own interest in nature stimulated. I lost this good possibility moreover, for bad motives — squeamishness and panic; and I justified it, at least in part, for a motive no better — the desire to be thought well of by my friends.

Sex

These aspects of my experience, I believe, are not unrelated to some aspects of abortion (if not specifically to the question of the significance of the fetus). Squeamishness, panic and a desire to be thought well of by other people — in other words, the desire for respectability — may be among the motives for seeking abortion. Abortion, that is, may be sought as a way of sweeping things under the carpet, or 'hoovering society', as one gynaecologist has put it. The desire for respectability may seem an unlikely motive for abortion. But despite society's apparent openness today about sexuality, the subject still causes a good deal of social embarrassment (partly because individuals' attitudes to it are unpredictable, partly because those attitudes may cover many different kinds of personal vulnerability, pain, anxiety and unconscious feelings). Certainly we are still far from the kind of society in which sex and sexuality are generally acknowledged as good gifts from God, which different people may enjoy and express in different ways, each guided by an informed and responsible conscience. In the absence of that kind of realism, society's mixed feelings still incline (even if rather less than in the past) towards linking sexual respectability with an idealised version of the nuclear family. That ideal, however, has at least as many ways of disappointing as of delighting people: but very often that is not easy for society or individuals to acknowledge frankly. If it were, perhaps we might be both more realistic about contraception and more prepared to support, psychologically and materially, some of the women who now seek abortion.

Squeamishness, panic and the desire for respectability, however, are only some of the motives in some cases of abortion. Other and better motives also may be involved and the circumstances of the woman may exert pressures which are difficult to resist, especially if her experience of life is limited. In this last respect, returning to my encounter with the spider, I am inclined to temper justice (which faults my motives) with mercy (which recalls that I was a small boy). However, leaving aside these considerations of motives and circumstances, what about the conclusion that I reached — that these were 'only spiders'? This raises the question, relevant I believe to the present theme, of our relations with the other creatures with whom we share the earth.

Jains

Some years after killing the spider, I read about the Jains in India, who scruple to kill any form of life, however small, gently brushing even the insects from their path. The Jains, and to a lesser extent other forms of Eastern religion, challenge a traditional Western assumption, which Christianity has not always discouraged, *ie* that humanity's God-given place in nature allows it to use and kill non-human creatures for whatever purpose it wants. Having read about the Jains, I soon discovered that the obvious retort to them is to take their view to its logical conclusion, and ask about the morality of killing those forms of life — disease-bearing micro-organisms — which threaten human life. The difficulty with this retort however, is that it covers only certain cases, and does not justify, for example, my killing of a pregnant spider which, as far as I know, posed no such threat to me. What right had I to kill a harmless creature for no good reason? None, as far as I can see. The incident may seem trivial enough, and the Jains may have little claim on the Christian conscience. Nevertheless the habit of killing non-human creatures for no good reason, we are now learning, is not without serious ecological consequences.

Killing and Evasion

Not everyone, of course, sees things this way. Much more recently, discussing the rights and wrongs of using human embryos in medical research, I asked a severe critic of the Warnock Committee's proposals if it was morally worse to use human embryos for this purpose than to use, say, adult dogs, cats or monkeys. 'I am not interested in animals,' he replied. 'You can do what you like with animals. What I am concerned about is preventing the murder of human beings.' This reply, I believe, was no more satisfactory morally than my own earlier conclusion about the insignificance of killing spiders. It begged the question, of course, of what 'murder' is, and I shall come back to this later. But it overlooked also the fact that killing is killing, whatever we kill, and that respect for human life can only be weakened if we have no respect for the other forms of life to which human life is related. One does not need to be a Jain, or to believe that animals have 'rights', to ask what justifies human beings when they erect a protective fence around the life of their own kind, and then claim that outside this fence they may kill wantonly and without good reason. One objection to that way of thinking, of course, is the historical evidence of it viewing even some sections of humanity as lesser breeds without the fence. But no less important an objection is based on some

of the very things which make human beings different from other animals —
in particular our special responsibility to care intelligently for created life on
earth. As human beings, in other words, we are answerable, and need to have
good reasons, for our actions towards other creatures as well as towards other
humans. But settling matters by deciding that these other creatures are 'only
spiders', or by saying that 'you can do what you like with animals', do not
sound like good reasons. What they sound like, rather, are ways of trying to
escape responsibility by evading the issue.

The fact that we may want to evade the issue in such ways, however, is
understandable. The issue, after all, is one which we have no entirely
satisfactory way of resolving. The underlying problem is that, in this world,
some killing and a great deal of 'allowing to die' seem inevitable. If some
creatures are going to survive, others must not. But which creatures should
survive when not all can? The rational, responsible ones — human beings —
often have the power to decide, and usually decide in their own favour. Yet
there seems no ultimately defensible reason, other than human collective
self-interest, why in any particular case a human life should be preferred to
that of any other living creature. As a species perhaps we may be more
necessary to the welfare of the world as it is now organised, but the same can
rarely be argued at the level of individuals. Nor does it seem reasonable to
claim that any human individual deserves more than any individual animal to
survive, simply because he or she is human. Jesus said, of course, 'You are of
more value than many sparrows'. But it is not clear that being more valuable
in God's sight entails a greater right to survive on this earth, if and when we
are in competition with other animals for earth's scarce resources. Our value
in God's sight certainly requires great respect for human life. But it does not
justify any lack of respect for the life of other creatures. Yet such lack of
respect we betray routinely as we use and kill other creatures for our human
purposes.

The Christian Gospel
What the transparency (and sometimes the vehemence) of our evasions
betrays then, is just how difficult it is for us to face up to the fact that our role
in nature is morally ambiguous and morally indefensible. We aspire to
become more rational and responsible, but in doing so discover how much we
remain kin of the beasts of prey. Animals with a guilty conscience, we are
reluctant to acknowledge our true position too frankly. Instead, in this as in
other matters, we use up our energies in trying to defend morally impossible
positions, generally making excuses for ourselves and trapping one another in
our self-absorbed anxieties. It is just this predicament, of course, that the
Christian Gospel seeks to turn into our possibility. It invites us, that is, to
acknowledge frankly that our position indeed is morally indefensible, and

that the Creator has always known this to be the case. Such an acknowledgement is the precondition necessary to set our energies and our intelligence free from self-absorption. Only thus are we free to consider how, in practical ways, we can exercise our responsibility more rationally, by doing the best that we can. The acknowledgement implies a shift from concentrating on whether or not *I* am doing the right thing, to concentrating on the problem itself, to which we may be able to make some limited, but useful contribution. Acknowledging our own moral indefensibility is not easy. Nor is it easy to understand why the Creator has put us in this position, which is not all of our own making. Such a painful acknowledgement, the Gospel teaches, is sustainable only in an awareness of the mystery of the lamb slain from the foundation of the world. In an awareness of that mystery (however little we comprehend its depths) we begin to be set free, so that we may play our limited part in moving creation closer to the vision of the lion lying down with the lamb.

The Gospel, I am suggesting, shifts our attention away from the question of whether or not I am doing the right thing, to the question of how we can do our best to contribute to God's good purposes. Even with the guidance of the Holy Spirit, the Bible and the Church, of course, this is no easy question, since the good purposes of God reach their fulfilment only beyond the horizon of our understanding. In practice therefore, there will be times when we can have little certainty that our best really is contributing to these purposes: there will be times also when doing our best in one way is possible only by doing less than our best in others; and times again, when we cannot really work out what is best. But despite these difficulties, the important thing is to keep on trying and trusting — trying to see the particular problem in as many of its dimensions as we can, trying to listen as attentively as we can to the voices of the Bible, the Christian tradition, reason and experience, and trusting that God, who is merciful, will achieve his good purposes through us, despite us and beyond us.

2 The Embryo and the Fetus

Against this general theological background then, let us turn to the particular question of the moral significance of the embryo and fetus. (The new life growing in the womb is normally called an embryo *before*, and a fetus *after* the stage when it becomes recognisably human — at about the eighth week of pregnancy.) What do the Bible and the Christian tradition tell us about this? What do we learn from reason and experience, in particular the observations of scientists and the arguments of philosophers? And in what different dimensions should this be seen?

The Bible and the Christian Tradition

The Bible does not say very much with direct reference to the embryo and fetus. For many people however, Psalm 139 provides an evocative text: 'thou didst form my inward parts, thou didst knit me together in my mother's womb ... my frame was not hidden from thee, when I was being made in secret' (vv.13, 15). This text, clearly, sees God wonderfully at work in the creation of a human being and inspires respect for the new life in the womb. But what does this respect imply as far as our attitudes towards that life are concerned? In particular, what degree of protection, against what threats, should we afford to embryonic or fetal life at its different stages? This kind of text does not give us this kind of information. Nor should we expect it to: we might as well seek criteria for infanticide in the last verse of Psalm 137.

A more directly relevant text perhaps, is found in Exodus chapter 21, which prescribes penalties for men who, while fighting, accidentally cause a woman to have a miscarriage. In the original Hebrew text, the relevant penalties were graded according to the amount of 'harm' done to the woman. But when the text was translated into Greek (in the third century BC) 'harm' became 'form'. This allowed it to be interpreted according to a different ancient legal tradition which graded such penalties according to whether or not the new life had achieved a human form. Subsequently, the Christian Church took over Aristotle's view that the new life did not become distinctively human until it was formed into a human shape by a human animating principle, or rational or intellectual soul. This was believed to take place at around 40 days after conception, before which the life was animated by principles comparable to those animating first vegetable, and then, later, animal life. The distinction based on formation, animation or ensoulment was used, in Church law, again to grade penalties for abortion.

The moral significance of this distinction was clearly recognised in the Christian tradition. St Augustine, the Church's most influential theologian after St Paul, did not believe that killing before about 40 days after conception was murder or homicide, *ie* killing a human being. Up to this point, he wrote, the life involved was 'some sort of living, shapeless thing ... not yet endowed with its senses'. St Thomas Aquinas, the greatest mediaeval theologian agreed: 'In the generation of man first comes a living thing, then the animal, and finally man ... the intellective principle is the formative principle defining man as a species'. This seems to have been the standard view in the Church until the nineteenth century. The point, it must be emphasised, is not that the Church ever regarded abortion as anything other than wrong; but until about 40 days it was *not* murder, it was *not* the killing of a human being.

In the nineteenth century, however, this view was abandoned, for at least two reasons. The first one was that the Roman Catholic Church was alarmed because modern medical techniques were making early abortion safer and thus more common. To close any possible loophole which might excuse such abortions, the Church declared that the traditional distinction made no difference to the seriousness of the act. It did not go as far as to declare officially that a human soul was infused at conception, and it remains permissible to hold the traditional view. But the effect of the nineteenth century change was that thereafter the Catholic Church tended to regard each human life as beginning at conception.[1]

Scientific observations
A second reason both prepared for and strengthened this view. Techniques of observing the embryo, improving from the sixteenth century onwards, made Aristotle's distinction seem much less significant: the scientific evidence increasingly pointed to the view that embryonic and fetal life, albeit passing through different stages, was an unbroken continuum. At no point in this continuum did any single biological change seem of sufficient significance to bear the weight of the traditional distinction. And in any case, to the modern mind, including that of many Protestants, the traditional language about souls and when they were 'infused', or when they 'animated' the new life, had become highly problematic, if not meaningless. Conception, the 'moment' when sperm and egg fused to form a new life, seemed the only single change of sufficient significance to make a moral difference. This conclusion was further strengthened when it was discovered, much more recently, that the genetic blueprint for the growing life is present from the first day after conception.

Viability
Such now seems the only commonsense view to many people, including many who defend the medical practice of abortion. Those who defend it, however, often prefer to emphasise the significance of the legal distinction (although not recognised in Scots Law) based on 'viability' — *ie* when the fetus becomes capable of life independent of its mother, albeit not without special care, at somewhere around 26 weeks. However, almost all medical abortions, except for the gravest reasons, take place before about 20 weeks and most of these before 12 weeks. Nevertheless a significant proportion again of these are performed after 40 days, and in terms of the traditional distinction would be interpreted as killing a human being. That, one suspects, may be among the reasons why some defenders of medical abortion find it sufficient to rest their case on the legal distinction, and prefer not to get drawn into moral and theological arguments the terms of which they find no longer very plausible.

Implantation

Although the view that 'human life begins at conception' is widely held, some scientific evidence suggests that this belief is not as simple and obvious as it may seem. There is, for example, the observation that conception is not a 'moment' but a process, including not only the fertilisation of the egg by the sperm, but also, about six days later, implantation of the fertilised egg in the mother's womb. It is possible therefore to interpret implantation as the completion of conception, and hence as the decisive end of the beginning. This interpretation is obviously helpful to those who are willing to accept contraception but not abortion, especially since the intra-uterine contraceptive device works by preventing implantation from taking place.

Fertilisation

Against this view, however, most Roman Catholic authorities tend to refine their position simply by referring to the 'moment' of fertilisation as crucial. But even fertilisation, it now appears, is a process, taking place over the 24 hours between penetration of the egg by the sperm and the time when the genetic information from each source is finally merged. The fact that fertilisation itself is a process, some feel, strengthens the view that one should not emphasise it as the morally crucial, definitive beginning of a new human life. The beginnings, rather, stretch back into the life of the egg and sperm. It seems disproportionate to claim that the respect and protection owed to the life of the fertilised egg should be so dramatically greater than that due to its component parts only hours before.

Natural Wastage and Experiment

This last consideration, for many people, is further strengthened by the observation that, in a few cases, fertilisation may result in the dangerous hydatidiform mole, and that in many others it may produce genetically defective life-forms which have no potential for further human development. Nature's need to eliminate these may be among the reasons why so many fertilised eggs fail to implant. The proportion is variously estimated, but at least half of all fertilised eggs seem to be lost in the natural process. To those looking for clues in nature, this high rate of natural wastage might suggest that the pre-implantation stage should be regarded as continuing the earlier natural experimental or sorting-out process, in which before fertilisation vast numbers of sperm also are lost. Further support for this way of looking at things, moreover, might be drawn from the observation that until about two weeks after fertilisation, the fertilised egg can divide into twins, or twin eggs can combine. Not until after this time, it can be argued, does the development of a stable individual embryo properly begin.

Philosophical Arguments

None of this scientific evidence, clearly, is sufficient to disprove the philosophical argument that the life of any existing individual can be traced back to the completion of his or her (or his or her actual or vanished twin's) genetic blueprint on the first day after fertilisation. Such a person may feel fully justified in claiming that because the potential for his or her life was already there, then all such potential (some say, actual) human lives deserve as much respect then, as they will do later, after birth. They deserve this, indeed, all the more, because, of all human beings, they are the most weak and vulnerable. This last point, surely, has some claim on the Christian conscience. The difficulty with this argument, however, is that it would seem to imply, if we are to be fair, that no less respect should be accorded to all the embryos lost in the course of nature. To many people, there seems something inherently improbable in this judgement.

Probability

A different way of looking at the matter might be to take the question of probability more seriously. In the days before it was appreciated just how many eggs were lost in the course of nature, a Roman Catholic theologian observed that there was 'an enormous shift in possibilities' between the prospects of sperm and those of a fertilised egg. Thus, he argued:

> As life itself is a matter of probabilities, as most moral reasoning is an estimate of probabilities, so it seems in accord with the structure of reality and the nature of moral thought to found a moral judgement on the change in probabilities here. At the point where the conceived being has a better than even chance of developing, he is a man.[2]

The point about this argument then, for those who still accept it, is that the 'better than even chance of developing' would now have to be moved forward from fertilisation to some time between six and 14 days after fertilisation.

Sensory Awareness

This argument also is not without problems. Many people will agree that once a healthy individual embryo is set on a course which, under normal conditions, will result in a healthy birth, its life ought to be respected. In this context, probability does seem a reasonable basis on which to argue. On the other hand, should the degree of respect at this very early stage be as great as is implied by 'he is a man'? To many people, the problem again is that this seems improbable. An important fact contributing to this is that the embryo cannot experience pain or have any sensory awareness until the nervous system has developed, which does not happen before six weeks after pregnancy. While it may seem mere coincidence that six weeks is very close to the mediaeval 40 days, the scientific evidence also at least suggests that the fertilised egg will develop through stages with characteristics which in some ways are comparable to those of vegetable and animal life, before distinctively human characteristics emerge. On the other hand, of course, this growing life has, all along, a human potential which plants and animals lack; and this surely makes some moral difference.

Personhood

The improbability inherent in claiming full human rights for the fertilised egg will seem even greater if a quite different kind of philosophical argument is accepted. Some people believe that only 'persons' have full human rights. The whole idea of rights, respect and protection, they argue, makes sense only to 'persons' — beings who have some awareness of past and future, and the capacity to value their own lives. 'Persons' form the 'moral community' whose members (in principle at least) recognise various reciprocal rights and duties towards one another. The characteristics required for personhood and membership of the moral community exclude animals (except possibly a few of the highest) and also infants, who are at best only potential persons. For many people, of course, the difficulty with this argument is that it proves too much. They might find it improbable to equate an embryo with 'a man'. But they would be reluctant to accept the conclusion of the personhood argument (in some versions at least), that under certain circumstances infanticide may be as permissible as abortion. Defenders of this conclusion, on the other hand, may reply that the difference between a late fetus before birth and an infant after it, is not really so great. Judged only by the human characteristics of the fetus and the infant, the difference between abortion and infanticide may not be as obvious as it seems.[3]

Poles and Lights

Some people then, believe that full human rights are acquired at conception, or at latest when 'the conceived being has a better than even chance of developing'. Others hold that only persons with a capacity to value their own lives have full human rights. These two views stand at the two poles of the debate about abortion, the former seeming to demand rescue of endangered fertilised eggs, the latter seeming to allow infanticide. Both, clearly, cannot be right, even if each can be made to sound very logical within its own terms of reference. Their respective terms of reference, however, point to a similar limitation in both, which may help to explain why many people in the middle of the debate find neither extreme view very satisfactory. The limitation is that of what has been called using a moral spotlight rather than a moral floodlight. Each of the extreme arguments, that is, focusses its attention on only a limited number of morally relevant features of the potential or actual human being, and bases its claims on these. But other features, which the moral spotlight does not illuminate (and a moral floodlight would), may be no less morally relevant.

Relationships and Commitments

Among these other morally relevant features are relationships and commitments. Rights may make sense only within the moral community. But denying protection to the fetus (and possibly the infant) because it lacks the full human rights of a person, ignores the relationships and commitments which are already drawing it into the moral community. On the other hand, claiming full human rights, and absolute protection, from conception, ignores the relative lack of relationships with and commitments to the fertilised egg at this early stage. It ignores also the relative moral significance of existing relationships and commitments whose claims may conflict with those of the fertilised egg.

The significance of existing relationships and commitments is most obvious perhaps in the now rare cases when the life of the fetus and that of the mother are in direct and immediate conflict. In this context, the Roman Catholic Church forbids direct killing of the embryo or fetus, even to save the life of the mother, arguing that the two lives are each equally entitled to protection. The fact that the Catholic Church, while sometimes uneasy about the implications of this position, seeks to uphold it, is some indication of its awareness that to concede its position in this case may open the way to further concessions. If one is allowed to kill the embryo or fetus in order to save the mother when the two lives are in direct and immediate conflict, it may then be argued that abortion is permissible in order to reduce the physical and mental strains and stresses of an 'unwanted' pregnancy, which also may lead to the mother's death, albeit over a much longer period.

Necessity and its Interpretation

The Roman Catholic Church's apprehensions in this respect are well founded. Killing an embryo or fetus to save the mother's life may be regarded as a necessary evil. But this does open the way to other claims that killing is necessary to avert other evils; and how are these to be judged? One traditional view of necessity is that the evil to be averted by killing must be greater than the evil of killing, and that killing must not be resorted to if there are less evil ways of averting the greater evil feared from allowing the pregnancy to continue. But in practice such judgements will be subject to many interpretations; and once one leaves the security of the ethical principle which the Roman Catholic Church seeks to uphold, much will depend on the judgement and integrity of fallible and sinful human beings.

Stages of Commitment

Unless we are prepared to uphold full human rights from conception then, we inevitably become involved in judgements about the relative seriousness of different evils. These judgements will be complicated moreover, if one takes into account the relationships and commitments which can be seen as already drawing the new life into the web of the moral community. The relationships and commitments involved are of different kinds. At implantation, for example, not only does the probability of the embryo eventually becoming a person increase, but also the mother's womb draws the embryo into a new and stronger relationship. The development of sensory awareness, again, marks the earliest beginning of a capacity not only for feeling pain and pleasure, but also for relationship. At quickening, around 12 weeks, the mother (whatever the philosophers might say) may begin to think of the new life as a person. The relationship normally is strengthened further as birth approaches; and a moral commitment to care for the baby seems so obvious that if, after birth, the mother fails to carry it out, society takes up the relationship's responsibilities.

Growing Protection

In these different ways then, it may be argued, the mother's and society's commitment to the new life is gradually strengthened, and it is gradually drawn within the moral community's web of relationships. In practice, of course, individual mothers may not make or acknowledge some of these commitments, and some societies have not done so either. They are, nevertheless, now sufficiently normal and common for it to seem reasonable to argue that the degree of respect and protection owed to the embryo or fetus should increase with the commitments normally undertaken towards it. To avoid making this judgement too subjective, the increasing probability of a normal birth through the succeeding stages of embryonic and fetal life, should be regarded as no less significant reasons for increasing respect and protection. As this probability increases and as commitments are undertaken, so the reasons for killing an embryo or fetus should be required to be correspondingly serious.

An Uncomfortable Conclusion

This way of arguing, I realise, will not easily convince those who take their stand at or near either of the poles of the debate about abortion. Not least among the reasons for this is that it cannot conclusively determine in advance which reasons for abortion are sufficiently serious to judge it necessary at which stage. The considerations it offers, rather, have to be weighed in the balance, case by case, and alongside all the other relevant considerations of motives, circumstances and consequences. This way of arguing acknowledges

hat killing ultimately is never justifiable, although it may be judged necessary
or reasons from the regrettable to the tragic. One purpose of arguing in this
way, indeed, is to underline this, in the hope of encouraging reflection on
these case-by-case decisions and greater consistency among the relevant
judgements. Such reflection, it is also hoped, may encourage all involved in
abortion to ensure that if it has to be performed, it should be performed as
early as possible; and that all possible ways should be sought to prevent the
necessity of it being performed at all. This way of arguing undoubtedly leaves
us in an uncomfortable moral position. But that, surely, is the position we are
in, and in which the Christian Gospel asks us to do the best we can.

Notes to Paper 4

1   The classic papers on which this account relies are G R Dunstan, *The moral status
of the human embryo: a tradition recalled, Journal of Medical Ethics* (1984), pp 1,
38–44 and J F Donceel, SJ *Immediate Animation and Delayed Hominization,
Theological Studies* 31 (1970), pp 76–105. Also important is: J Mahoney, SJ, *Bioethics
and Belief* (Sheed and Ward, London 1984).
2   The quotation is from J T Noonan, Jr, *Abortion and the Catholic Church: A
Summary History, Natural Law Forum* 12 (1967), p 129, cited in G L Hallett, *Christian
Moral Reasoning* (University of Notre Dame Press, London, 1983).
3   On the subject of this paragraph see J Harris, *The Value of Life* (Routlege and
Kegan Paul, London, 1985) and M A Fox *The Case for Animal Experimentation*
(University of California Press, London, 1986).

Response to Richard Higginson

Richard Higginson's paper is in two parts. The first part discusses whether the fetus is a person, the second whether it is always wrong to kill persons. The second part is largely an application to abortion of traditional arguments about 'double effect' and the 'just war'. To be of practical help, these arguments require us to be pretty clear about the intentions, guilt and innocence (not the opposite of guilt but the non-harming character) of the different parties. In cases of abortion this is much more difficult to be clear about than Richard Higginson implies. More complicated also than he suggests are judgements about threats to the life of the different parties. The threat of a further pregnancy to the life of a mother with several existing children, or in poor health or social circumstances, may be no less real for not being immediate. By focusing the argument on immediate conflicts, and by assuming that intentions, guilt and innocence can be established clearly, Richard Higginson excludes many of the moral considerations which make actual decisions about abortion so difficult. The clarity and consistency of his argument, in other words, is achieved at the cost of comprehensiveness. And in the end, of course, the relevance of the arguments in the second part of his paper depends on whether he has established, in the first part, that the fetus is a person.

In the first part of his paper, Richard Higginson argues that no age or stage of development after fertilisation is sufficiently different from that which goes before it, to be taken as the point after which personal status should be ascribed to the embryo or fetus. On the other hand, the 'gradualist viewpoint', which also recognises that there are no 'decisive moments', is insufficiently 'objective'. Thus, 'in view of the unsatisfactory nature of the alternatives', personal status has to be ascribed from fertilisation. There are, I believe, three serious objections to this argument.

The first objection is that the argument underestimates the significance of the shift in probabilities (mentioned in my own paper) which takes place around the time of implantation. This raises problems for Richard Higginson's argument because a similar shift in probabilities (albeit on a larger scale) is among the reasons commonly advanced for regarding fertilisation as crucial.

The second objection is that while none of the 'alternatives' to fertilisation (or at least, implantation) is sufficient *on its own* to justify a decisive change in status, the point about the 'gradualist viewpoint' is that many people adopt it after considering how all these biological and psychological factors, *taken together*, tilt the balance of the moral argument. The 'gradualist viewpoint' moreover, generally holds that the moral argument is not just about the rights of the embryo or fetus, but also about responsibility for the consequences of *not* making the always tragic choice to end a pregnancy.

The consequences of not aborting, of course, would weigh much less heavily in the moral balance if it could be shown conclusively that personal status should be ascribed from fertilisation. But the third objection is that Richard Higginson's argument does not do this. However much he wants to be 'objective', he admits that the moral question could only be finally settled if we knew 'how God sees early embryos'. But this is precisely what we do not know. Rather, we have to draw our own conclusions from what we know, on the one hand about God, and on the other about nature.

The conclusion which Richard Higginson draws is that, at the very least, we should 'give to this possibly personal creature the benefit of the doubt'. But in the light of our knowledge of nature (in particular the possibility of a pre-implantation natural 'sorting-out' process suggested in my paper), the gradualist way of giving the benefit of the doubt would seem more plausible than the absolutist. Even on the theological assumption that God does see each embryo as a person, moreover, it does not necessarily follow that God's intention for each of these is a life on earth at this stage in human history.

A final theological question is that of what weight we should give to maxims like 'giving the benefit of the doubt' or (as Richard Higginson puts it in another context) adopting 'the oft-recommended approach' and erring 'on the side of caution'. The biblical God confers not only human dignity, but also human responsibility. Exercising human responsibility (as the parable of the talents, for example, suggests) does not always mean erring on the side of caution. On the contrary, it may mean that, having taken into account all the circumstances and contingencies of a particular moral choice, we have to take the risk of acting without total certainty that what we are doing is right.

Response to Kenneth Boyd

I have enjoyed reading Kenneth Boyd's thoughtful and sensitive paper. There are many points on which he and I agree. We are largely agreed on our reading of the Christian tradition and on empirical data about the fetus — although I think that he is wrong to cite 12 (compared with my 18) weeks as a typical time for quickening, and an increasing number of premature babies born before 26 weeks do survive. But I am particularly grateful to him for relating the issue of abortion to the question of respect for animal life. I would certainly disassociate myself strongly from his adversary who argued, 'You can do what you like with animals'. I believe that we should have a high regard for animal life, and I am myself a vegetarian.

Yet I do not agree with Dr Boyd's judgement that, 'there seems no ultimately defensible reason, other than human collective self-interest, why in any particular case a human life should be preferred to that of any other living creature'. The Bible clearly indicates that human beings, as creatures made in God's image, are of greater value than the animals, and therefore, when the well-being of man makes this necessary, animal life may be taken. Animals do matter to God, and so casual disregard for animal life (as evidenced in animal sports, or their use in research connected with the cosmetics industry) is definitely wrong. But the idea of a hierarchy of creation suggests that where research on animals is closely related to human *medical* needs, it is permissible. The same cannot be said about research on humans, even tiny ones.

Dr Boyd goes on to stress the ambiguity and indefensibility which characterise moral existence in general. Here I am reminded of an alleged remark by Paul Ramsey, when irritated by a fellow American ethicist who was disavowing all clear-cut ethical positions: 'You're one of these Protestants for whom everything is too damned ambiguous!' Neither Ramsey nor I would dispute that moral judgement is often a delicate and difficult business. But emphasising ambiguity (a stress often accompanied by talk of 'grey areas') can be a cloak for abdicating responsibility to work out, as best one can, what is the morally best solution. This is not a fair criticism to make of Dr Boyd, on the evidence of his paper, but it is characteristic of many who adopt the gradualist position. And what does make me uneasy, paradoxically, about Dr Boyd's view is his apparent conviction that if one feels uneasy over a moral judgement this helps to put the action which one has approved in a better light. The implication is that awareness of unavoidable guilt makes certain acts of abortion excusable. Better in most cases, I would say, to avoid the guilt by not consenting to the act of abortion.

On the specific issue of the status of the fetus, I am largely content to let readers make their own comparison of Dr Boyd's views and my own. Most of the objection which he lodges against regarding fertilisation as a crucial developmental point have been anticipated in my paper. I am intrigued by the view which he still regards as too rigorous: that personhood should be attributed when 'the conceived being has a better than even chance of developing'. How can a statistical variable either side of the 50 per cent mark *determine* anything so momentous? Is a cricketer to be credited with the status of being a batsman on the basis of whether he has 'a better than even chance' of scoring 50? Is a Member of Parliament to be credited with the status of being a politician on the basis of whether he or she has 'a better than even chance' of becoming a government minister? The cricketer may be dismissed cheaply; the MP may drop out of politics; the embryo may die; but as long as they are involved in the developmental process, we should give them credit for what they are.

Dr Boyd believes that once one concedes that abortion may be justified in order to save a mother's life, this 'opens the way' to arguing that it is necessary to avert other evils. After all, the strains and stresses of an unwanted pregnancy may lead to the mother's death over a much longer period. I find this reasoning unconvincing. One might equally well argue that the unexpected guilt which can follow having an abortion might also have a long-term lethal effect. The fact is that in the vast majority of cases, a clear distinction can be made between threat to life and threat to health; doctors know when a pregnancy poses an imminent threat to life. If it does, then the life of the mother (usually the only life which can be saved) should rightly be the paramount concern. If the threat is less severe, then we are not comparing like (the life of the fetus) with like (the health of the mother), and if the personhood of the fetus is acknowledged, its rights to exist should be protected.

The gist of Dr Boyd's argument is that personhood is linked to the involvement of the fetus in a network of relationships and commitments. He shows sensitivity to the charge that this makes the judgement too subjective, but I think that the criticism still holds. With a law as vague as the one which now prevails, a fetus which has the misfortune to be growing in a mother who refuses to acknowledge these relationships and commitments is in mortal danger. More fundamentally, why should the status of the fetus depend on how other people *feel* about it? Personhood is not conferred on human beings by other human beings. It is a God-given *datum* of existence which is either there at a certain point or not there. While I have admitted that we cannot be absolutely sure that it is there at the earliest moments of an embryo's existence, I am convinced that it does not depend on the fickle nature of a particular parent and a particular society's sense of responsibilities.

5

The Church's Traditional Teaching About Abortion

Introduction

The point of this brief paper is not the satisfying of historical curiosity. Rather, it is to contribute to an understanding of the morality of abortion: whether abortion is, or is in particular circumstances, something which should be carried out, or which may be carried out, or which is not to be carried out. But if our central concern is, as it is in the whole collection, to consider whether abortion is, or, depending on circumstances, may be, right, permissible or wrong, can a survey of historical teaching and attitude contribute to this concern?

Many will say something like this: from the fact that people of the past held some view about what should or may or should not be done over some issue, we can deduce nothing about the correct moral stance on that issue. Even if these people of the past approach the matter on the basis of general principles for behaviour which we also accept, and speak unanimously, we cannot agree to their moral conclusions simply on their say so. If we are to be responsible, we must see for ourselves that there are reasons which justify us in our view. And even if it is these people of the past who by their writings help prompt us to recognise justifying reasons for our moral conclusions, then these conclusions must rest on the justifying reasons and not on any moral authority of the ancients. There will be some who see this as a particular application of the maxim that no 'ought' follows from an 'is'. So from some historical fact on its own, no moral conclusion can flow.

The relevance of traditional teachings to modern discussion may also be questioned by pointing out that there are significant differences between the issues addressed by the traditional teachings and the issues about abortion as they confront us: we can often predict with a known probability that a particular fetus will, if it comes to term, be deformed, diseased or be otherwise abnormal; we can carry out abortions with much less risk to the life of the pregnant woman; we know a great deal more about conception and about the earliest stages of the life of the fetus. Partly for these reasons there

66

are particular questions about abortion which did not occur to earlier Christians to reflect upon, but which trouble us. So, even if the earlier reason for doubting the value — for a discussion of morality — of a survey of the traditional teaching on abortion is set aside, these changed factors lead people to think that when we discuss the morality of 'abortion', we are discussing a set of circumstances or a number of questions so different from those which the traditional teaching was discussing, that the traditional teaching is, or is largely, irrelevant to modern concerns.

In the face of such widely heard claims, it will be necessary, in what follows, to give attention not only to facts about the Church's historical teaching, but also to indicate ways by which a survey of these facts can assist our moral reflection.

There is little scope for disagreement about the Church's traditional explicit teaching. Admittedly the Scriptures seldom deal with abortion in a way that is uncontroversially direct (so, for example, it is a matter for controversy whether 'Thou shalt not kill' applies to the issue of abortion); and where they are direct, as at Exodus 21:22–25, the exact import of what is said has been in dispute and is disputable. However, the early Church does quite explicitly and directly, and repeatedly over the whole post-scriptural period (and into the Dark Ages and then the Mediaeval Church) deal with abortion. There are several competent surveys of this (*eg* Bonner, Braine, Gorman)[1] with which it is unnecessary to attempt to compete here, (and on which the present writer could not improve), both because of their easy availability and because there will surely be general agreement with Professor Bruce Metzger's judgement: 'It is really remarkable how uniform and how pronounced was the early Christian opposition to abortion'.[2]

It seems that amongst those having a claim to be regarded as responsible theologians it was not until the fourteenth century that a feeble flicker of dissent from this consensus flickered.[3] In our own century, many more voices have been raised in dissent against the traditional view, but there is also a very substantial concurrence with the traditional view in, *eg* the writings of Barth and Bonhoeffer.[4] In what follows, I shall discuss the teachings of the early Church, to try to draw out something of its significance. (Later writers, by giving fuller argument for their views, make their point rather more clearly for themselves than the earlier Church.)

There can be little doubt that the overwhelming weight of Christian tradition has been against abortion, and even those who most vigorously question whether the traditional teaching can have import for contemporary moral debate are obliged to attend to the reasons which the tradition has offered for its view. The Christian writers of the past were, after all, not completely in error over what they took abortion to be, nor were they fools;

and it would be a presumptuous modern who supposed, without a sympathetic look at what they said, that they *all* resisted the Holy Spirit's leading.

One of the earliest statements of the common Christian stance sets the prohibition of abortion next to prohibition of infanticide: The *Didache*[5] says 'You shall not kill the child in the womb or murder a new-born infant'. Infanticide, like abortion, was advocated and practised in the ancient world; these practices were advocated by political thinkers and statesmen (*eg* Plato, Augustus Caesar) as a means of population control for the good of the state, and practised for these reasons and reasons more immediately personal, such as the elimination of illegitimate children whom it would be inconvenient to bring up or who would undesirably complicate inheritance settlements. Against this background, and sometimes against accusations that Christians actually practised infanticide, the Church repeatedly condemned and disciplined those who practised either infanticide or abortion.

Particularly in Roman times, the Stoic teaching, which held the fetus to be part of the pregnant woman's body, was widely influential. Only at birth, or, more accurately, when it drew its first breath, did it become a distinct human being. The Christian stance against abortion is a stance against this Stoic position, which appears to have informed Roman Law, and Roman social attitudes more widely. In *its* (penitential) law the Church is consistent in regarding abortion as wrong.

The Stoic teaching did not imply the 'woman's right to choose', however, and, quite widely, it was the father's wish in the matter which was held to be paramount; so if a woman secured an abortion for herself without her husband's wishing it, she was held to have offended against him, *ie* to have 'cheated' her husband. Indeed, whether the underlying thought was Stoic or not, the father was held in both law and morality to be entitled to dictate whether an abortion should or should not take place, so that when Christians spoke on behalf of the fetus, it was against fathers' rights that they were pressing.

Greek philosophical culture sometimes attempted to distinguish between a formed and an unformed fetus; a formed fetus has a soul (whether this is thought of in Platonic — as was more common — or in Aristotelian terms) and its death was regarded as being the death of a human being. Judaism, as it was influenced by the Septuagint, interpreted Exodus 21:22–23 as employing this distinction and as treating the destruction of the formed fetus as murder. Against this, St Basil affirms that the formed/unformed distinction 'is not admissible amongst us'. And Augustine appears to have thought that the formed unformed distinction, although perhaps conceptually defensible, had little application because it is impossible to say *when* the unformed becomes formed. This appears to have contributed to Augustine's condemnation of abortion; he also condemns abortion as the improper sundering of procreation from sexual intercourse.

The foregoing is a brief account of the context and point of early Christian teaching about abortion; it is, of course, to a degree selective, but the selection is not eccentric and any reader who doubts that it sets out fairly the main features of early Christian teaching about abortion may consult the further surveys referred to. Suppose it is accepted as a fair sketch, how does it bear on our modern moral concerns?

It has to be conceded that, as far as we can discover, several questions which are of concern to us were not discussed much, or even at all, in early Christianity, and were certainly not the subject of an explicit wide consensus. May fetuses about whom (or which) it is known with certainty, or an established probability, that they will be defective or diseased, be aborted? Is abortion permissible when conception was the result of rape? Does the use of *aborti facients*, which act on the fertilised egg in the first hours after conception, constitute an acceptable method of birth control? On these issues we can only try to infer the Church's likely attitude; we may then consider whether the Church's reasoning, as so inferred, commends itself to us.

Of course, one reason for the early Church's silences on questions about hard cases is that it had first to assert its general opposition to abortion against the prevailing attitudes and practices which have been sketched in Section I. Compared to the urgency of that need, a rather low priority was attached to the need to pronounce on the relatively small number of hard cases; and perhaps the modern Church should consider for its part whether it devotes so much time and attention to debating hard cases and having its debates heard by the general public, that the greater need effectively to assert a general opposition to abortion is neglected. The present writer attended an Open Meeting of the Glasgow Medical Group in 1974 at which the Professor of Obstetrics and Gynaecology in the Royal Infirmary declared that, in his unit, what was in practice abortion on demand, had been carried out for years; and he saw no reason to change. If that policy is widespread (happily, it is not universal), and if modern Christians agree with their predecessors about the serious and general wrongness of abortion, it seems that the Church could and should, and spiritedly, make much clearer what it does affirm.

The repeated juxtaposition in early Christian writing of abortion and infanticide, at once serves as a corrective to some recent modern Christian discussion and prompts the asking of questions which are highly pertinent to our moral enquiry. Let me explain. Recently acquired knowledge about conception, and the earliest stages of whatever it is that exists shortly after fertilisation has occurred, have focused a great deal of attention on that early phase. Not only has the Warnock Committee been necessary, and its views discussed, but many Christian debates about abortion have centered on the question of whether or not from conception there exists a human person, who should be treated as such; and earlier attempts to distinguish formed from unformed fetuses have come to seem amateurish. But most clinical abortions take place when the fetus is several weeks old, and there are useful questions to be asked whose reference point is birth rather than conception. Early Christians were in as good a position to consider these questions as we are, and by what they wrote they can serve as a corrective to our tendency to focus on conception. So, for example, they prompt us to consider whether, as they appear to deny, there is some morally significant difference between an infant and a fetus at the age at which most clinical abortions actually occur. This is, surely, a central question to address, if we wish to consider the justifiability of clinical abortions which are carried out after pregnancy has been confirmed, and if we have a view on the justifiability of infanticide. Moreover, it is a question which troubles those who are, or are under pressure to be, involved in the practice of abortion and who know at first hand the characteristics of an aborted fetus — what it looks like, how well advanced towards babyhood it is. Yet, although the addressing of this question ought surely to be a first priority both in providing an answer to the most obvious of our moral problems, and in giving needed pastoral help, it is addressed rather seldom.

Perhaps it cannot nowadays be taken for granted that infanticide will be rejected by all Christians. The ancient practice, opposed by the early Church, of exposing 'defective' infants (*ie* leaving them to die of exposure and starvation) is difficult to differentiate morally from the withholding from a 'defective' infant of drugs which would probably cure pneumonia which it has developed; and yet there are modern Christians who appear to approve such a policy on occasion. But by its practice of Infant Baptism, the Christian Church appears to be committed to a high view of young children, whom Christ embraced, blessed, gave priority to, in his kingdom and protected by uttering dire threats against any who do them harm. Certainly all of this sits ill with any notion that it is the fully developed adult (whatever she or he would be like) who is to be valued, and that a child is to be respected only because it has the potential to develop into such a full person. ('Unless you become as little children ...') *Prima facie*, Christians will be opposed to infanticide, and will not appeal to a lack of potential in a particular child for full, mature man-or-woman-hood as sufficient reason for withholding available means to life. And, of course, quite without doubt and hesitation most Christians abhor infanticide. If the Christian attitude to children is correctly indicated here (and time fails me to discuss whether this attitude requires further rational support, and, if so, whether such is forthcoming, and to discuss particular hard cases which arise in the practice of paediatrics), the early Church's utterances imply that what goes for children goes also for fetuses whose known presence might cause someone to seek abortion. The challenge is thus set before those Christians who think that abortion may be permissible, to explain wherein fetuses significantly differ from infants.

The Stoics, as we saw, thought that independence in physical detachment from the mother is determinative of the existence of a distinct person; current British law appears to favour, rather, possession of the capacity to live in physical detachment from the mother (*ie* being 'viable'). An advocate of the early Church's view might ask whether the importance which is assigned, by Stoics or British legislatures, to physical detachment is sensibly assigned. (Suppose a pair of Siamese twins is born and allowed to develop for a time before a medical judgement is sought as to whether, perhaps by the donation of required organs and modern transplant surgery, the twins may live physically separate lives. If it turns out that they cannot ever reasonably hope to do so, we shall hardly think ourselves by this development now entitled to treat one 'twin' as merely a dispensable part of the other's body!) A new-born baby remains dependent, in many respects, on others; the new ways by which, after birth, its needs have to be met do not appear to be in themselves a justification for attaching a different status to a fetus (viable or not) and an infant. If the new ways by which an infant's needs are met — or a viable fetus's needs may be met — are treated not as significant in themselves, but as marking other significant discontinuities, the person who would treat fetuses differently from infants must tell us what these discontinuities are. A survey of recent writers who do attach a different status to a fetus and an infant shows that most either ignore the question or answer it in a way which lacks force. If the question is not satisfactorily answered, then the affirmation of fathers' rights (such as a Roman might have expressed) or of women's rights (such as is more likely to be expressed today) can only justify abortion if fathers or women are entitled to kill infants. And fetuses conceived in rape will be permissibly aborted, only if infants conceived in rape are permissibly killed, unless the question can be satisfactorily answered.

And if it is claimed that there must be a distinction between fetuses which have developed to the point of having the status of a person and those which have not yet reached that point, St Augustine's apparent response to the attempted formed/unformed distinction seems cogent still. He appears to say that because we cannot be at all confident how the distinction is to be drawn, and since a consequence of drawing the line in the wrong place may be action which is morally equivalent to murder, we should not rely on any such possible distinction, but abjure abortion altogether. Whether or not that was precisely St Augustine's thought (it may also have been St Basil's), he prompts us to reflect on the enormity of the moral risk, the risk that what we are doing should count as a fearful offence. In turn, that prompts us to consider how a risk of bringing about some avoidable unhappiness is to be weighed against the great moral risk that we commit what is equivalent to murder. Surely this is a line of reflection which is worthy of respect and further discussion. Does it not place an onus on those who consider abortion to be permissible in certain circumstances to justify themselves against it?

Conclusions

Although there are some modern questions about abortion to which early Christians made little contribution, there is enough in these early writers to raise important questions: What is the difference between an infant and a fetus which is old enough that its presence is known in the standard ways by which women know themselves pregnant? What justification is there for taking the great risk of acting on the basis of doubtful distinctions between that which has become a human person and that which has not yet done so? Early Christian tradition proposes the answer 'none' to both questions. If it is correct in this, most of the modern moral questions about abortion to which early Christianity did not address itself need hardly be considered. And those modern Christians who think that the early Church was wrong in saying 'none' to these two questions, and so condemning abortion, must show *why* it was wrong. In leading us to this point a study of the early Church teaching assists our moral reflection without removing our autonomy in moral judgement. And whether that autonomy really does matter much is a question for another occasion.[6]

Notes to Paper 5

1   G Bonner, 'Abortion and Early Christian Thought' in *Abortion and the Sanctity of Human Life* (edited by J H Channer) (Paternoster Press, Exeter, 1985), pp 93-122.
David Braine, *Medical Ethics and Human Life* (Palladio Press, Aberdeen, 1982).
M J Gorman, *Abortion and the Early Church* (Paulist Press, New York, 1982).
2   ibid, p 9 (Metzger's Foreword).
3   John of Naples and Thomas Sanchez are examples. For details see J T Noonan's own article in *The Morality of Abortion: Legal and Historical Prospectus* (edited by J T Noonan) (Cambridge, Massachusets, 1970).
4   K Barth, *Church Dogmatics* (English Translation) (T and T Clark, Edinburgh, 1961) Volume III, Part 4, pp 415ff.
D Bonhoeffer, *Ethics* (English Translation) (Collins, London, 1964), pp 175-176.
5   With which the Epistle of Barnabas, Athenagoras in his *Supplication for Christians*, Tertullian, and other known authorities, agree.
6   I have been assisted in writing this paper by David Braine and by Ian Hazlett; they are not to be held responsible for such use as I have made of their help, but I am grateful to them.

6

Abortion: Christian Traditions Not Unanimous

Introduction

There are a number of different sets of questions that may be asked about abortion, and I distinguish four sets of such questions:

(1) *Legal questions*, such as: What is the law on abortion in Scotland or any other country?

(2) *Legal-moral questions*, such as: Does the law on abortion enshrine any moral rules, principles or values?

(3) *Moral questions*, such as: Is abortion ever morally justified? If so, in what circumstances and for what reasons?

(4) *Moral-legal questions*, such as: What ought the law to be on abortion? Ought abortion, if morally justified in certain circumstances, to be made legal in these or some of these circumstances? What safeguards (*eg* against abuses, such as 'back-street' or indiscriminate abortion) should the law provide?

Here we are concerned primarily with the third set of issues — (3) above — although how we answer these will of course depend upon how we answer the second set of questions — (2) above — and the fourth set — (4) above. We shall have occasion to look at the history of the law on abortion, as that has often indicated the moral views held by Church and society.

A further restriction in this paper consists on commenting on the moral issues only as they arise from the history of the various Church traditions. There are, however, certain problems in interpreting the traditions on which we desire to comment.

What are the questions that we are addressing to the various Christian traditions? These are obvious candidates:

Does this tradition justify abortion in any circumstances?

If so, what are the circumstances, and for what reasons?

Are these reasons theologically and morally acceptable to Christians today?

With our greater medical knowledge and resources today, can these reasons be restated in terms that are acceptable medically, morally and theologically today?

If at times this tradition does not justify abortion in any circumstances, can we discern why the Church at that time was so inflexible in its attitude?

Can we be sure that this tradition was so inflexible? Perhaps when it denied abortion, it did not have the range of cases that a person today has in mind?

When we list the questions like this, we begin to see that we cannot hold a simplistic view of the task of interpretation, as if all we had to do was to read the documents to find out what any particular Christian tradition had to say in answer to our questions today. What then can we expect from the tradition?

For us not to expect any guidance at all from the history of the Christian Church seems to me presumptuous, and a denial of 'the promised guidance of the Holy Spirit' in the past.

On the other hand, to expect the tradition to settle the matter finally for us in 1986–87 seems to me to be a form of escape from the exercise of our Christian responsibility in the present, where the traditions will be one factor, but only one factor, to be taken into account in making our decision.

Further, we cannot simply open the books of the tradition to know what it was even saying in *its* day, let alone what it is saying to our day. Words in *any* text always need to be interpreted, and the more we are concerned with a text from a different culture to our own, the more difficult the task of interpretation becomes. We have to learn to read 'the sub-text' that underlies the text. Indeed later generations may understand *the same words* quite differently from the generation that first produced the text. For example, in Shakespeare's '*Tempest*' Act I, Scene 1, the words of the mariners — 'All lost! to prayers, to prayers! all lost! — mean to most people today, 'Let us ask God to save us from drowning, for prayer is the only resort we have'. But in Shakespeare's day they meant, 'We are about to die. Let us make our peace with God'.

There are two obvious factors to be taken into account when interpreting a text from the past. First, what was the context then in the past? For example, when abortion appears to be being condemned outright, it may be that the ancient author associated abortion solely with sexual immorality and the desire to conceal a pregnancy after illicit intercourse. He may never have had in mind a therapeutic abortion to save the life of the mother, or an abortion after rape, criminal assault or incest. His apparent outright condemnation of abortion may turn out to have been a condemnation of a restricted range of cases.

Second, by what key concept was the Christian life understood? Was it by means of law and commandment in the sense of an order from a superior, or was it by means of freely-given, joyous response to God's grace? Was the Christian life conceived as obedience to a set of rules controlling outward behaviour, or as involving a response of one's entire being, encompassing motive, intention, disposition, virtue and character? Was it conceived in terms of a set of principles that allowed for no exceptions on the grounds of justice or compassion?

A History of the Christian Tradition

1 *The First Five Centuries*

From the earliest times, Christian opinion was strongly opposed to abortion, which was a serious social evil in the first and second centuries *anno Domini*, and the Church did its best to prevent Christians simply imitating the ways of the world. No one familiar with the history of Christian ethics in the early centuries will be surprised at this opposition to abortion, for the legalistic strain found in later ethical strands in the New Testament was continued in the early centuries, where there appeared to be no understanding of the priority of grace over law. In the *Didache* and *Doctrina*, the Christian life is interpreted as conforming to law; how else than by teaching fairly concrete rules to be observed by all, could their teachers 'make concrete their sense of obligation to their neighbour and their understanding of the Christian life in the face of the ethical assumptions of the Jewish and Greek worlds, not to speak of the necessity to safeguard the faithful against the perils of anti-nomianism and paganism'? At any rate, cultural factors played an important part in the progressive over-emphasis on rules, and by the second century the process was well advanced. The *Didache* has been described as 'practically devoid of any reference to grace received, or continuing experience of God'[1], while *Barnabas'* rules–ethics 'would have satisfied the most devout rabbi'.[2] In other words, later New Testament ethics, like the ethics of *Didache* and *Barnabas*, are increasingly time-conditioned.[3]

Not only do the *Didache* and *Barnabas* condemn abortion, but Clement of Alexandria (*c.*AD 150–*c.*215) in the *Tutor* was typical of his time in associating abortion with sexual immorality and in prohibiting the use of drugs to induce an abortion. In a similar vein, Tertullian (*c.*AD 160–*c.*221) condemned abortion to hide a pregnancy, and his contemporary, the African lawyer, Minucius Felix, denounced 'women who, by medicinal draughts, extinguish in the womb and commit infanticide [*parricidium* = strictly murder of a parent or other close relative] upon the offspring yet unborn'. One suspects that this apparent wholesale condemnation did not cover some of the cases taken to be morally justified by some Churches today.

One is not sure what to make of Tertullian. He is often cited as occupying a highly important, if not special, place among early theologians in unequivocally equating abortion with murder. In his *Apology* for the Christians (*c.*AD 198), written before his love-affair with Montanism, he replied to a charge of infanticide, being levelled against Christians, by affirming that Christians will not even entertain abortion:

But to us [*sic* Christians], to whom murder has once and for all been forbidden, it is unlawful even to destroy the fetus in the womb whilst the blood is still forming into a human being. Prevention of birth is premature murder... That also is a human being, which is about to become one, just as every fruit exists already in the seed.[4]

It sounds clear enough, but one wonders whether he was carried away by his own rhetoric, for in his *De Anima*, he calls abortion to save a woman's life a 'necessary cruelty' — cruelty, no doubt, but evidently permissible, and not then murder.

Despite being the father of Latin theology, Tertullian was something of an 'odd-ball'. In his later years, he spoke in favour of Montanism, which taught the imminent end of the world and the need, in view of this, for greater austerity in living: no more marriage, longer fasting, no flight from martyrdom. He had very peculiar ideas about what constitutes Christian behaviour in other ways: *eg* one was not to wink nor to cross one's legs. The thought is bound to occur to any Christian today: if he were as time-bound as that on those issues, how far can we trust him on abortion?

Tertullian, however, is important in the history of the tradition in the West on the issue of abortion, as he taught a view of the soul quite different from the one later accepted from the time of Aquinas for many centuries. In the *De Anima*, chapter IV, he argued that the soul came into existence with the body at birth. It is, therefore, created by God and is not the result of the process of procreation. On the other hand, again, we are aware of how time-bound he is when he teaches that this soul has a corporeal nature, for it can suffer in hell, and suffering implies a body that can feel the pain!

About 100 years later, the same strict view on abortion was being advanced. In the West, the Council of Elvira (*c*. AD 300) decreed that a woman guilty of an abortion should be refused the sacrament, even if she were dying. In the East, the Synod of Ancyra (modern Ankara) in AD 314 relaxed the life-long exclusion from the sacrament to a ten year penance for such a woman. St Basil in a letter written in 374 wrote:

A woman who deliberately destroys a fetus is answerable for murder. And any fine distinction as to its being completely formed or unformed is not admissible amongst us.[5]

Thus Eastern Orthodoxy has through the centuries, following Basil the Great, refused to accept the distinction between the formed and unformed fetus, or the ensouled and unensouled fetus, that became orthodoxy in the West for centuries.[6] St Basil, however, accepted the ten year penance decreed at Ancyra, but added that the period should be determined not by its length, but by the nature of the repentance. (In the East, however, the moral legitimacy of direct abortion to save the mother's life is not entirely ruled out.)

By the time of Augustine, however, this rigorous position had been somewhat relaxed, and abortion was considered allowable in certain circumstances. This change coincided with a change in the relation of the Church to society, once Constantine declared the Roman Empire Christian. As long as the Church had a minority status, and it was necessary to nurture first-generation converts in the Christian life, amid the lax morality associated with paganism, it was understandable that rules, conceived of as admitting of no exceptions, should be framed for their guidance. But when the Church became a majority movement, it was understandable that the Church's position should become somewhat less rigorous.[7] Such a change seems to have been demanded by the time of Augustine of Hippo, and this as we shall see became the position of the mediaeval Church.

2 *The Mediaeval Age and its Doctrine of Natural Law*

This change depended, too, on a different doctrine of the soul than that taught by Tertullian. Augustine denied that the soul came into existence at birth but at a certain point in fetal life, later known as the moment of 'quickening', when the mother felt the child make a movement in the womb for the first time. This doctrine of the soul later received classic expression in the theology of Thomas Aquinas. Following Aristotle, he taught that every living organism, be it vegetable, animal or human, has a soul (*anima*), *ie* the active, moving principle, and the substantial form, of the body. The human soul or *anima* is not transmitted with the semen, but is created by God. This divine creation of the human, rational soul, however, takes place, not at birth, but at a certain stage in the development of the fetus.[8] This was after 40 days from conception, and for centuries the Church saw this 'animation' or 'ensoulment' as occurring at some point after conception, usually identified as between the thirtieth and fortieth day for males, and between the sixtieth and eightieth for females. This was based on an understanding of Aristotle, not on biological knowledge. Prior to this human 'ensoulment', the fetus possessed only an animal or sensitive *anima*, and indeed, for the first few days after conception, only a vegetable anima. While quickening was at first thought to be distinct from 'animation', eventually the two came to be identified in law and so in the popular judgement.

Abortion before 'ensoulment' was regarded less seriously, although it was still condemned — partly because any interference with procreation was regarded as wrong. Such, at any rate, was the understanding of natural law, which may have been a misunderstanding of Aquinas.[9] For example, Thomas Sanchez SJ, an early seventeenth century moral theologian, thought abortion of the unensouled fetus legitimate to conceal adultery, but only provided the woman's life was in danger and not just her honour, were she to be discovered. Acquinas himself, however, seems to have had some insight that in some circumstances there can be a conflict of duties or of values — between the value of the mother's life and that of the fetus. He paraphrases Paul in Romans 3:8, saying that 'evil should not be done that good may come', and from this concludes that 'a man should not kill the mother in order to baptise the child'.[10]

In 1591, Pope Gregory XIV restricted the penalties respecting abortion to those involving the animated fetus. Before such ensoulment, and certainly in the first 40 days, therapeutic abortions (to save the mother from death or danger to her health) were considered justified and their legitimacy continued to be debated in official Roman Catholic circles until 1895.

The Common Law in England reflected this official Church view, both before and after the Reformation. Abortion was a crime, and was treated as if it were a form of homicide, but the law allowed therapeutic abortion before ensoulment. A similar tradition prevailed on the continent of Europe, as a result of the moral teaching of a large number of leading theologians, notably Antonio Pierozzi, who was canonised in 1523 as St Antoninus, and who permitted therapeutic abortion before animation or quickening. A similar view was taken by other leading Catholic moral theologians in the period from the fourteenth to the seventeenth century, including John of Naples, Giovanni Andrea, Dr Navarrus, Diego Covarruvius of Levya, Enrique Henriquex SJ, Dom Graffius OSB, Vincenzo Filiucci SJ, and Paul Laymann SJ.

In the nineteenth century abortion began to be controlled by *statute*, instead of the Common Law, with severe penalties for those procuring an abortion after quickening. The first such statute in 1803 was known as Lord Ellenborough's Act and made abortion a felony without benefit of clergy and thus punishable by death. This was meant to tighten up the law and make it more clear, in response to pressure from the medical profession. It did not, however, achieve these goals, for it proved difficult to decide when a mother's quickening had taken place. The old distinction was still embodied in the statute, but later legislation removed it.

While the absolutist stand taken by modern Popes against abortion is a recent phenomenon, when considered against the backdrop of history, the way was being prepared for such an absolute from the seventeenth century onwards, when the doctrine of the inviolability of nascent life began to take shape. This was to become the cornerstone of the Roman Catholic position from 1869 onwards. Thus in his 1679 decree, *Errores doctrinae moralii laxioris*, Pope Innocent XI condemned:

(1) the practice of abortion even before animation, when the motive was to spare the pregnant girl death or shame;

(2) the erroneous doctrine that every fetus lacks a rational *anima*, so long as it is in the womb, and that it only begins to have a soul at the time it is born;

(3) the view 'that no homicide is committed in any abortion'.

Despite this, the distinction between the animated and the unanimated fetus continued to be central in Roman Catholic discussion of abortion until the eighteenth century, with theologians discussing what considerations might justify abortion and override the value of fetal life, particularly before ensoulment: the factor most frequently advanced is when the mother's life is in danger, but the protection of her health and reputation are also put forward.

3 *The Roman Catholic Church from 1869 onwards*

The Church's view changed in 1869, when Pope Pius IX removed any reference to a distinction between an animated and unanimated fetus, and thereby, according to most interpreters, laid down the present doctrine of the animation of the fetus *at conception*. Pope Pius IX set excommuncation as the penalty for those seeking to procure an abortion. The official teaching (until recently at least) became that the fetus is a human person, or is to be treated as if it were a human person, from the moment of its conception. Abortion, therefore, is always contrary to God's intention, and is simply murder. This is the official position of the Roman Catholic Church today, reinforced in the strongest terms by Pope John Paul II, although several moral theologians within that Church question the wholesale condemnation, as we shall see. At the root of this internal controversy is the whole question of how moral theology carries out its task and what is the key concept by which the Christian life is to be understood — *viz* law or response, relation and love — or, in other terms, shall we give priority to grace over law?

Why did the change take place at that time? By 1869 the medical profession could no longer support the distinction between the quickened and unquickened fetus and so the parallel 'theological' distinction between the animated and unanimated fetus had also to be abandoned. The change was due as much to advancing medical knowledge as to movements in theological understanding. The reproductive process was becoming better understood: the ovum was only discovered in 1827 and the woman's role in reproduction was, in consequence, being seen differently. The Church's position moved with that of medical science to seeing *conception*, and not *ensoulment*, as the decisive moment.[11] Abortion therefore, *in all circumstances* was condemned by successive papal decrees of 1884, 1889, 1902, 1930 and 1968. The decree of 1902 condemned abortion even when the fertilised ovum was developing outside the cavity of the uterus, such as within a Fallopian tube. In 1930, Pope Pius XI decreed as follows:

'The infliction of death, whether upon mother or upon child, is against the commandment of God and the voice of nature: "Thou shalt not kill!" The lives of both are equally sacred.'[12]

He described medical and therapeutic indications for abortion as merely excusing, but not justifying, 'the direct murder of the innocent'.

The Second Vatican Council in 1965 adopted an equally absolutist position:

'The varieties of crime are numerous: all offences against life itself, such as murder, genocide, abortion, euthanasia and wilful suicide ... debase the perpetrators more than the victims and militate against the honour of the creator'.[13]

It also declared in the context of marriage:

'Life must be protected with the utmost care from the moment of conception: abortion and infanticide are abominable crimes.'[14]

We cannot be certain, however, that Vatican II would have said anything different in the case of abortion, say, in a case of rape outside marriage.

Pope Paul VI's encyclical *Humanae Vitae* in 1968 condemned abortion even for therapeutic reasons.

Despite the absolutist position of the present Pope — John Paul II — there are three indications that *in practice* the Roman Catholic Church is not as strict as its pronouncements might make us think. First, several moral theologians within that Church have discarded the model of law that lies behind this kind of authoritative pronouncement. Bernard Häring writes:

On questions of morality, the role of infallibility is limited to the enunciation of the most basic principles, to declaring, for instance, the fundamental right of man to life and prohibiting unjust killing.[15]

Häring means that there is a difference between adhering to the principle of unjust killing, and holding that *all* acts of abortion *without exception* are wrong. Many moral theologians would see Häring's position as evincing a faithfulness to what Aquinas had to say on natural law, and the absolutist one as a betrayal of Aquinas. Two years earlier, in 1970, Edna McDonagh wrote that we are no longer tied to a juridical and inflexible approach and that, 'no longer free to reach for his manual to find the answer to a particular problem, the Catholic student of moral theology finds himself confronted with a bewildering range of information, analysis and opinion on an increasing range of problems'.[16]

Second, moral theologians have instanced some circumstances in which an abortion would be justified: for example, the removal of an ectopic pregnancy, and the sacrifice of a fetus, when this is incidental to, and not the main purpose of, an operation to excise a diseased organ. This would be a case of indirect abortion and an instance of the principle of double effect.[17] Some authorities even allow for dilatation and curettage within a few days after a case of rape, on the supposition that conception may not have taken place.

Third, it is well known that, in this country, Roman Catholic mothers have long practised forms of artificial contraception and have used the abortive facilities that the State provides. Priests cannot be, and are not, ignorant that such practices are common, and obviously modify — and are encouraged to modify — the rigour of the official position in their pastoral ministries. Despite the present Pope, the overall Roman Catholic position on abortion is not static and does respond to social change.

4 Lutheran, Reformed and Anglican Traditions to the Present Day

Both Luther and Calvin held that both soul and body exist immediately at conception, and so did not have the distinction between animated and unanimated fetus. The status of the fetus was of primary interest to the Reformers with regard to the doctrines of creation and predestination. Luther does not appear to have discussed the issue of abortion, although he spoke of the child in the womb as having a soul. It is likely, then, that Luther rejected abortion outright. Calvin certainly did. In his *Commentaries* — see Genesis 38:10 — Calvin called abortion 'an expiable crime', and in response to Exodus 21:22 he comments that 'the fetus enclosed in its mother's womb already is a man'.

It is, however, very dubious as to whether we have any right to quote this in support of an absolutist position. Was Calvin ruling out all the instances of abortion that come to the minds of people today when they consider whether there are not some circumstances where an abortion might be justified: *eg* to save the mother's life, to remove a cancerous growth, when the child in the womb is likely to be severely handicapped, mentally or physically, or when an unmarried girl has been raped? In Calvin's day, some of these motives had not been thought of: the normal motive was *thought to be* to conceal an unwanted pregnancy, occurring after illicit sexual intercourse. Further, therapeutic reasons would not be in people's minds then, nor recognised by the medical profession whose surgical techniques were not advanced enough: *eg* an abortion in the sterile and antiseptic conditions of a modern hospital was not available. In the seventeenth and eighteenth centuries both Anglican and Puritan divines condemned abortion, because they usually (perhaps always) associated it with sexual immorality and they sometimes used the distinction between the formed and unformed fetus, so that they allowed abortion before ensoulment.

When we come to the twentieth century, we find the mainstream Protestant traditions diverging sharply from the official Roman Catholic position, although not so much from the practice of that Church. They place more weight on the special or unique circumstances of each abortion decision and on the responsibility to decide of those involved, especially the mother.[18]

'Often the conflict inherent in abortion is acknowledged by calling abortion tragic and ambiguous, even when morally warranted.'[19] While abortion is a serious matter in these traditions, only to be morally justified in special and relatively infrequent circumstances, Christians in them are readier to support abortion when the pregnancy has resulted from a clear act of injustice (*eg* rape, criminal assault, incest), when it gravely threatens the physical or mental health of the mother, or when the fetus is seriously abnormal, and when the abortion can be performed early in pregnancy.

While this is, I believe, an accurate resumé of the general trend in mainstream Protestantism, when we turn to individual theologians, we find examples of all the three main positions possible on the issue, *viz* absolutist, non-absolutist and mediating positions. The treatment of their viewpoints will serve as a convenient introduction to a final discussion of the issues arising from this historical survey.

The absolutist position was represented by Dietrich Bonhoeffer. He held that (a) the embryo's existence is itself evidence of God's intention to create a human being; (b) the embryo's right to life is, therefore, divinely bestowed; and (c) any deliberate deprivation of its life is 'nothing but murder'.[20] This is a form of natural law doctrine, as that doctrine came to be misunderstood in traditional moral theology after Aquinas.[21] God's will is merely a postulate inferred from observation of nature,[22] *ie* that procreation has begun. This is to abandon all responsibility for decision-making in every abortion situation, on the ground that 'nature's way' is always 'God's way'. As against this, we may ask whether nature's way is God's way in cases of rape, criminal assault and incest. Such an argument as Bonhoeffer's rules out the use of *all* forms of contraception in *all* circumstances, with the exceptions of complete abstinence, the 'safe period' and *coitus interruptus* — the traditional Roman Catholic position on that issue. Human values are simply read off 'nature': what is right to do simply corresponds to 'nature'. Anything which alters or interferes with the course of nature is an unwarrantable intrusion which is morally objectionable.[23] If 'nature is always to take its course, then I should have died many years ago when my general practitioner intervened in my pneumonia by administering for the time [the medication] "M&B 693"'. We cannot forego direct, intentional and caring interference with natural processes. Professor George Newlands in commenting on Bonhoeffer's position on abortion[24] reminds us of what G E Moore wrote in his *Principia Ethica*:

> If everything natural is equally good, then certainly ethics, as it is ordinarily understood, disappears; for nothing is more certain from an ethical point of view, than that some things are bad and others good; the object of ethics is indeed, in chief part, to give you general rules whereby you may avoid the one and secure the others. What then does 'natural' mean in this advice to live naturally, since it obviously cannot apply to everything that is in nature?[25]

We may take Helmut Thielicke as representing a mediating position. He based a modern understanding of sexuality on the Lutheran 'orders of creation' of which for him marriage was one, although because of Paul's doctrine that marriage signified the mystical union that exists between Christ and his Church, Thielicke saw it as in the order of redemption as well. Human beings, however, transcend nature and should responsibly intervene in nature, by modifying, developing or improving 'natural' processes, so that contraception in an over-populated world can be God's will. Thielicke cannot, therefore, accept the form of natural law doctrine put forward by Bonhoeffer. The sanctity of human life, and so its inviolability, are established at fertilisation. This sounds like an argument from nature, especially when he defines the inviolability of nascent human life by the claim that 'the fetus has its own autonomous life' because it has its own circulatory system and brain — a claim difficult to make of zygote, embryo or fetus at any stage. But he does not hold a naturalistic ethic or an absolutist position, for he allows for the possibility of therapeutic abortion, on the ground that God's will cannot be equated with the world as it is (*eg* war and disease) — it almost sounds like a criticism of Bonhoeffer's position — but he fails to clarify in what circumstances such abortions are justified.[26]

Karl Barth exemplifies the non-absolutist position. For him 'the divine grace always has priority, the human response is one of obedience. Gospel always comes before law, never law before grace as in the Lutheran order ... Hence there is no question of either natural law or the orders of creation being independent sources of moral guidance apart from the Gospel or the grace of God in Christ'.[27] Barth had a second reason for ruling out all generalised norms, including the Lutheran orders, as independent sources of guidance, *viz* his view of the divine freedom. 'No law, no set of rules, not even the law in the Old Testament or in the New, can encapsulate the freedom of God who speaks to us in a way always consonant with that divine freedom. The command of God, therefore, is not a generalised command, but a particular command to me in my situation.'[28] So for Barth 'human life, and therefore the life of the unborn child, is not an absolute'.[29] In all circumstances, a responsible calculation is to be made before God, and sometimes we shall consider an abortion justified. We cannot always tell in advance that we have made the right decision, but we must proceed, confident of God's forgiving grace. In the nature of this position, it was not open to Barth to specify the circumstances when an abortion would be justified.

In the twentieth century the Church of England has been influential in achieving various 'liberal' changes in the law (notably on homosexuality and suicide), and so in 1965, in view of the public debate on abortion, the Church of England Report, *Abortion: An Ethical Discussion*, was published. It was hoped that this Report would have an influence on the legislation likely to be enacted as previous Reports had had. The Report suggested that a pregnancy might be terminated if the 'health and well-being of the mother [a term used to denote psychological as well as physical health] were endangered', but insisted that conception as a result of rape or criminal assault, or the risk of fetal deformity be not accepted *as grounds* for termination in themselves, but that they be considered *circumstantially* as factors affecting the health of the mother, the diagnosis and prognosis of which should be *one* factor determining medical decision.

But the Abortion Act 1967 (which came into force on 1 April 1968) virtually ignored this advice. The provisions for Scotland are the same as those for England and Wales. Instead it both made the grounds for termination wider and attempted to define the limits of legality which can be summarised in the following way.

Termination was to be legal where:

(1) the continuance of the pregnancy would involve risk to the life of the pregnant woman, or of injury to her physical or mental health, or of any existing children;

(2) and there is substantial risk that, if the child were born, it would suffer from such physical or mental abnormality as to be seriously handicapped.

And this is where we are today. Our immediate concern in the Church of Scotland is with the consequences of that legislation and subsequently their likely consequences for embryo research. There is evidence of widespread dissatisfaction, not only from the Churches in our land, but also from some sections of the medical profession and the general public. Professor G R Dunstan of the Chair of Moral and Social Theology at King's College, University of London, in commenting on the 1967 legislation, writes: 'There is at present widespread disquiet at the number and distribution of abortions effected under the terms of the Act'. [30] Others might speak of 'discontent' or even 'horror' at the interpretation placed on it by some surgeons. It is always wise to look at an issue on a global scale, if we can: it may balance our distortion or myopia. But instead, on this issue, we find our worst fears realised. 'More than half of the world's population now lives in countries where abortion is available for medico-social reasons as well as purely medical reasons. [31]

Termination is increasingly available, here and elsewhere, for medico-social reasons, which seem easily to shade off into reasons of the personal convenience of the parents. Failure of contraception and the determination not to have a child appear to combine and result, or are suspecting of resulting in resort to termination, On the other hand, world food resources will not sustain, we are told, a population increasing at the present rates in

Africa, India, the Far East and other places, and so in many lands there is increasing pressure from governments and other agencies to resist the number of births by all means possible.

B Summary and Conclusions

Behind this immediate concern with current legislation and its working in practice lies our concern with whether abortion is ever morally justified.

The guidance that we receive from the Christian centuries is that abortion is always a serious matter, only to be justified in special and relatively infrequent circumstances, and for adequate medical, moral and theological reasons. This rules out the two extremes: that no abortion can ever be so justified, and that all abortions are always so justified. On the one hand, no Christian Church can ever go with the abortion 'on demand' lobby, or agree that terminations should take place simply for the convenience of the parents. For the Christian, human life, even in the case of the embryo and fetus, is to be respected, because such life is given by the Creator and because God became incarnate in a human life in Jesus Christ, our Lord and Redeemer. On the other hand, 'respect for human life' cannot be erected into an inviolable principle, *ie* one that admits of absolutely no exceptions. In any case of termination, there are two lives to be respected and there is a conflict of values from which this so-called inviolable principle does nothing to deliver us. If instead we go even further and make 'the inviolability of the fetus' an absolute, we have, as it were, cooked the books in advance of the auditors' visit, as if we were trying to distract their attention away from other matters — in this instance, away from what is to be done if the mother's life is at serious risk, if it is a case of conception after rape, criminal assault or incest, or if the fetus is seriously abnormal. As for 'letting nature take its course', I have already shown that position to be untenable.[32]

If Christians are to talk of principles, there are two that have priority for them, on the authority of their Lord, *viz* justice and mercy, 'the weightier matters of the law'.[33] In some cases these are the questions that should be uppermost: *eg* 'has the cause of this pregnancy been the mother's reception of unjust or unmerciful treatment, and will the allowing of it to go to full term be another unjust or compassionless act?' and 'will this pregnancy (in the case of a cancerous tumour) result in the mother receiving unjust or unmerciful treatment?'.

Notes to Paper 6

1   K E Kirk, *The Vision of God* (1931), p 135.
2   J B Lightfoot, *The Apostolic Fathers I* (1890), Volume II, p 503.
3   Ian C M Fairweather & James I H McDonald, *The Quest for Christian Ethics* (1984), p 34.
4   Tertullian, *Apology*, Chapter IX.
5   St Basil, *Epistle* 188.
6   See below, pp 5–8.
7   Cf Robin Gill, *Theology and Social Structure* (London, 1977), p 48.
8   *Summa Theologiae*, 1a, qv 118, articles 1–3. Aquinas' account of human reproduction follows closely that of Aristotle in his *De Generatione Animalium*.
9   Fairweather and McDonald, *op. cit.*, pp 149–150, 152f.
10   *Summa Theologiae*, 3a, qv 68, article 11.
11   The new teaching could appeal to a minority view in the past, *eg* that held by Albert Magnus, Aquinas' teacher.
12   In the encyclical *Casi Connubii* (1930) the context makes it clear that 'child' means 'unborn child'.
13   'The Pastoral Constitution on the Church in the Modern World (Gaudium et Spes)' 7 December 1965: No.27 in *Vatican Council II, The Conciliar & Post Conciliar Documents,* General Editor Austin Flannery, OP (Dominium Publications, Dublin, 1975, 1977), p 928.
14   ibid, 51, p 955.
15   *Medical Ethics* (St Paul Publications, Slough, 1972), p 37.
16   *Doing the Truth* (Dublin, 1979), p 14.
17   Briefly, this principle states that an action which has a double effect, *ie*, both a good and a bad result, *eg*, the excision of a cancerous growth and the death of the fetus, may be performed, under certain conditions.
18   cf John Mcquarrie *et al, A New Dictionary of Christian Ethics*, p 5.
19   ibid, p 5.
20   D Bonhoeffer, *Ethics* (1955), pp 175f.
21   cf above pp 5f and p 8.
22   Harmon L Smith, *Ethics and the New Medicine* (1970), p 39.
23   Bonhoeffer refused even to recognise that sometimes there is a conflict of values — between the life of the mother and the life of the embryo. In a footnote, he affirmed: 'The life of the mother is in the hand of God, but the life of the child is arbitrarily extinguished'. The contrary argument, therefore, that intervention in nature is justified to save life, but not to destroy it, is not available to Bonhoeffer: intervention to save life is equally condemned.
24   *Making Christian Decisions* (1985), p 86.
25   G E Moore, *Principia Ethica*, pp 41f.
26   *The Ethics of Sex* (reprinted from his *Theological Ethics*) (1964) pp 227f, pp 242–5.
27   Fairweather & McDonald, *op.cit.*, p 182.
28   ibid.
29   *Church Dogmatics* (III/4, 1961), pp 416f and p 420.
30   G R Dunstan, *The Artifice of Ethics* (1974), p 37.
31   Supplement to the *International Planned Parenthood Federation News*, March 1972. This report was based on a survey of the legal status of abortion in 138 countries.
32   ibid, pp 11f.
33   See Matthew 23:23.

Response to Joseph Houston

Dr Houston and I share common ground which is far more important than our differences. We share a disquiet at the scale of abortions being effected in this country under the 1967 legislation — both with regards to their number and distribution and with regards to the range of reasons given for them. There is a similar trend in many countries which covers half the world's population. I am in agreement with Dr Houston when he writes (p 69): 'perhaps the modern Church should consider ... whether it devotes so much time and attention to debating hard cases and having its debate heard by the general public, that the greater need effectively to assert a general opposition to abortion is neglected'. There is no doubt that the Church has taken, over the centuries, a general stand against abortion. In view of the value given to children by our Lord in the Gospel and by the Church in our Sacrament of Baptism, there is no doubt that this ought to be the Church's general attitude.

Yet the hard cases remain, and the Church must consider whether compassion ever sets aside inflexible rules, and whether indeed in the Church grace must not take priority over law.

Section A

In this section I was to address myself to the question of whether there was need to clarify or amplify points brought out in my own article which I might feel have been inadequately covered in that of Dr Houston.

I wish to make two main points and then to add a number of reasons in support of these. First, whereas my paper attempted to sketch the whole history of the Christian tradition (or should I say 'traditions'?), Dr Houston has been somewhat more selective in his historical review, has relied almost exclusively on the early Church (roughly up to AD 500) and has appeared to treat the early Church's absolutist anti-abortion stand as normative for later centuries, ignoring or dismissing whatever in later centuries was not consistent with that standard. The distinction between the unformed and the formed fetus is a notable example of such dismissal. Admittedly, attempts to distinguish the two have come to seem 'amateurish', as Dr Houston holds and as the Church herself resolves. To this, however, there are three rejoinders:

(1) Are they to be considered 'amateurish' in the light of later medical knowledge, or because they do not conform to the norm of the early Church?

(2) If the former, why should the standard of modern medical knowledge and expertise not be relevant right across the board — both to our analysis of early views, proposed as they were, in ignorance of later medical knowledge and technology, and also to the modern debate? If the latter, on the other hand, why in the light of the Reformers, should the priority of law over grace

in the early Church not be considered theologically unsound and, therefore, ethically unacceptable?

(3) As long as the Church accepted the distinction between the formed and unformed fetus (a distinction admittedly medically amateurish) — and it was accepted for many centuries — the Church's testimony was *not* one of unbroken and complete opposition to abortion in all circumstances, an opposition which is arguably theologically unsound and ethically unacceptable.

Second, in making selective use of resources, namely the early Church (including St Augustine and St Basil), Barth (whom in the light of my article gets it only half right) and Bonhoeffer, and in devoting so much space (*viz* the whole Section 2 — which is almost exactly half his paper) to the modern debate (despite intermittent references to early Christian writing, the Stoics and St Augustine), he has produced a quite different article to mine. In rereading our remit I see that it was understandable and permissable to write that kind of paper, yet it is important to realise wherein the difference lies. He has a quite different balance of content from mine, because he has a different purpose and intention: he is more interested in advancing a point of view than in reviewing and analysing the sources in the whole Christian tradition from the first to the twentieth century, whereas, while I too support a point of view, I am more interested in doing justice to the latter. There is a place for each type of article and in some ways they are complementary to one another.

These are my two main points and I now adduce a number of reasons in support of them:

(a) Dr Houston has a tendency to use mildly tendentious phrases, which may suggest to the unwary reader that more may be claimed than the evidence allows. He opens his historic review with a sentence: 'There is little scope for disagreement about the Church's traditional explicit teaching'(p 67). This sentence is thus framed and located in the text to suggest perhaps that the evidence for the absolutist position against abortion extends beyond the early Church into the Mediaeval period. This, of course, is not so, as my article brings out. Yet this suggestion is further imprinted in the reader's mind by a subsequent sentence, *viz* 'However, the early Church does quite explicitly and directly ... (and into the Dark Ages and then the Mediaeval Church), deal with abortion'. This sentence may seem to suggest that the Mediaeval Church dealt with the abortion issue in the same way as the early Church, by advocating the absolutist position. Again, of course, this is not so. One of the books that Dr Houston recommends — J H Channer (Ed), *Abortion and the Sanctity of Human Life* — may be criticised on the grounds that it gives the impression that the absolutist no-abortion stand of the early Church is the only position that the Church has ever taken. Indeed, the chapter that he particularly draws our attention to, 'Abortion and Early

Christian Thought' by G Bonnar, is confined to the early Church — quite legitimately you may say, as that was its remit. However, it follows a chapter entitled, 'Using the Bible in the Debate about Abortion', and these two chapters are grouped together in the book under the heading 'The Christian Witness': nowhere is there any hint given that the witness of the Church has not always been to the absolutist anti-abortion position.

(b) Dr Houston makes selective use of Augustine. While Augustine condemned abortion, it was his distinction between the unformed and the formed fetus, along with the teaching that abortion before the formation of the fetus was not equivalent to homocide, which passed into Western Canon Law and remained there for centuries. Perhaps we should notice in passing that one of Augustine's reasons for condemning abortion — to which Dr Houston draws our attention — *viz* the improper sundering of procreation from sexual intercourse, is not one to which the reformed Churches, including the Anglican Communion, desire to give approval today. We do not hold that within marriage sexual intercourse must always be for procreation.

(c) Barth would not support the absolutist position as I make clear in my statement.

Section B

In this section I was asked to reflect on areas of disagreement. I confine myself to three:

(1) We agree on a general stand against abortion. We appear to disagree on the hard cases. Yet even on these Dr Houston appears to be ambivalent. On the one hand he seems to hold the absolutist anti-abortion position, yet he can write, 'Time fails me ... to discuss particular hard cases which arise in the practice of paediatrics'(p 70): this seems to allow for abortion in at least some hard cases. Had he developed this, he would have modified the position which he seems on the whole to espouse.

(2) Dr Houston makes much of the point that either abortion is equivalent to infanticide, or else we need to be shown wherein the difference lies by those who advocate abortion (presumably) even in *some* circumstances. Infanticide, or the murder of infants, involves the intention to kill, but where the surgeon tries to save the life of the mother by removing a tumour, and the unintentional result is the disruption of the fetus, then this kind of therapeutic abortion is not equivalent to infanticide. In other words, Dr Houston's argument fails to establish the absolutist anti-abortion position.

(3) In Christian ethics, if we are to speak of values at all, we cannot reduce all values to *one* value only, for there are a number of values to be considered — life, veracity, no-coveting, no-stealing, no-adultery, justice, love, mercy and compassion to name but a few. While as Christians the pre-eminent value

is *agape* or love, which unites all the other virtues, so that courage, for example, is a virtue only where it is exercised for the sake of others' interest or advantage. These values cannot be reduced to one and so there is always a possibility of a conflict of values in our decision-making. If one starts or ends an argument on abortion or on any other moral issue with one *sole* value to guide our moral judgement, for example the unalienable rights of the fetus to life, or, in other words, that it is always morally wrong to deprive the fetus of life, then not only do we rule out of court other values, such as justice and compassion, but we narrow down the value of life to the fetus only, and overlook the value of the life of the mother. This I do not regard as a tenable Christian position, and our horror at the scale of abortion being effected in Britain today must not be allowed to blind us to the ethical enormity of all one-value position. And so, one major area of disagreement between us centres around the question whether in this and other issues there is ever a conflict of values in our Christian moral decision-making, and whether *all* decisions are between black and white or whether *some* are between various shades of grey.

Response to Ian C M Fairweather

Any modern interpreter of ancient texts, which he has reason to respect, will advance hypotheses according to which texts say things to which the interpreter can give at least some approval. Thus, an interpreter of Plato will try to construe passages from Plato so that they do not say what is merely silly. The interpreter will make suggestions according to which what Plato said was, at worst, plausible; and if he can reasonably offer a reading agreeing with what Plato presents and what the interpreter sees as striking wisdom, he will do so. As Ian Fairweather and I discuss the Church's teachings about abortions, the differences between us arise much more because we differ over what is right to say about Christian morality in general and abortion in particular than because we differ about the plain force of these texts in themselves.

I agree with him that when a particular writer in the early Church period condemns abortion it is possible that he is thinking of circumstances quite unlike the 'hard cases' in which some modern Christians consider abortion to be justified. Against this, many of these 'hard cases' did present themselves to people of that early period, but there is no evidence (apart from the remark of Tertullian, who scorned consistency) that they were regarded as calling for qualifications of the general prohibition of abortion.

My claim is that powerful but frequently neglected anti-abortion arguments are at least suggested by early Christian statements when these are taken in their wider contexts. And my concern is that these arguments (their sources duly acknowledged) should be reckoned with. Given the available evidence, a demonstration is unlikely to be forthcoming that early Christians had no such anti-abortion arguments in mind. But even if that demonstration were to emerge, the force of the anti-abortion arguments would remain. Fairweather's *Summary and Conclusions* indicate acceptance of some of the implications of these anti-abortion arguments; but, inconsistently, some of the implications seem to be resisted, in the name of a selective justice and a partial compassion. But, before I turn to Ian Fairweather's *Summary and Conclusions*, his favoured themes from Christian tradition call for comment. He contrasts a life led according to the law and commandment of a superior, with a life of freely given joyous response to God's grace (pp 74 and 75 for example) as though these are exclusive alternatives. In view of Exodus chapter 20, where the 'Ten Commandments' are given to enable the people to respond to God's grace in leading them out of Egypt, and in view of Psalms 19 and 119, it is far from self-evident that these must be exclusively alternative conceptions of the Christian life. Perhaps Ian Fairweather would agree that his conception of Christian morality here is controversial but should plead, reasonably enough, that he lacks space to defend it fully.

One difficulty which this conception has to face is: How are Christians to be guided in giving their free joyous response to God's grace? (It may be said at once that 'guidance' would restrict or exclude freedom. For example, responding obediently to my wife asking me to shut my mouth when eating biscuits may be as *free* as deciding to shut my mouth without being asked would certainly have been. But it would be less spontaneous; and many people value spontaneity in personal relations. But is there not a conceit in supposing that we need no guidance in the eliminating of faults of which we are unaware, or which we underestimate, many of them more serious than uncouth, noisy biscuit-eating?) Having guidance will not diminish freedom, but it *will* diminish arbitrariness; and with this point we refer again to the difficulty of Ian Fairweather's stance, and refer to his *Summary and Conclusions*. In view of this difficulty which he faces in giving determinate shape and content to Christian living, it is somewhat daring of him to complain, against his opponents, that the adoption as inviolable as such principles as 'respect for human life' will not on its own deliver us from conflicts of values, so as to give firm guidance.

There are two important attitudes in the *Summary and Conclusions* which I welcome: (a) The rejection of abortion on demand (not, unhappily, a 'lobby' only, but an actual policy and practice — how widespread this might be is hard to know), and (b) the recognition that, 'In any case of termination, there are two lives to be respected' (p 85).

The latter attitude, if it is understood as following from the anti-abortion argument which I have brought out, appears to rule out any question of procuring the end of one life for anything less than the saving of the other from certain (rather than likely or possible) death, and perhaps it rules out even that. Yet conception by rape or incest is proposed by Ian Fairweather as a possible ground for termination, as is serious abnormality of the fetus. The justice and compassion which mothers certainly should receive in these circumstances appear to be being withheld from fetuses. Indeed, if there are two lives, having, as human lives, equal claim, why, if abortion may sometimes be permitted out of justice and compassion for mothers, may matricide not be occasionally permissible out of justice and compassion for the fetus? We recoil from the last suggestion. Why, if the fetus does have for us the same status as the infant and mother, should we not likewise recoil from abortion? In short, if, as Ian Fairweather suggests, there may be exceptions permitted to the principle of respect for human life, why is it that apparently only the fetus should be considered for 'termination'? This is simply to re-frame the question which my own paper asks: On what basis may we treat a fetus (of abortable age) differently from an infant which is to be treated as a human person?

I well realise that to pose that question is not to answer the practical questions about abortion which arise. It may even make the answering harder; and much more needs to be said. But the direction of this 'much more' must be shaped by our answers to this question which (as I maintain) the early Church raises.

7

Abortion From the Viewpoint of the Doctor Who Will Not Perform Them

My Reasons for a 'Pro-Life' Stand

I decided to specialise in Obstetrics and Gynaecology in 1967 — a fateful year. I was working at that time as a Medical Officer in Malawi, in Central Africa, totally unaware of the contents and implications for my future career of the Abortion Act which was going through Parliament at that time. I returned to England to continue my speciality training in 1970 and obtained a junior post in a Teaching Hospital in the North of England, little knowing that it had a reputation as 'the Abortion capital of the North'. I was not in favour of abortion but was prepared to 'terminate a pregnancy' where I could see no alternative way out of the patient's predicament. I quickly found that my 'conservative' attitude brought me into conflict with the Consultants over me. I was even told at one point that I would never obtain a Consultant post in that Region. As it was I obtained my Specialist Diploma in 1972 and returned to Africa. I took up a Consultant post at the newly opened Kilimanjaro Christian Medical Centre in Tanzania. My views on abortion had not changed when I returned to this country in 1978 but I quickly obtained my present Consultant position — in my old Region.

I began re-thinking my position on abortion after being in the post for some two to three years. I was made to think even more seriously about it by the advent of Francis Schaeffer's *Whatever happened to the human race?* I knew however, that saying 'no' to abortions would have many implications. I was concerned mainly that it would mean losing the chance to see and counsel women seeking abortion, several of whom might change their minds. There was also a question mark over the attitude of my employers. They in fact were quite prepared to accept my change of heart. I also knew that if I was to start saying 'no', then I had to be prepared to offer a viable and acceptable alternative, and that would be costly, in more ways than one.

Why did I change my mind?

It is often assumed that when doctors qualify, they signify that they will work in accord with the Hippocratic Oath. I have never seen the Oath in its entirity. I do know that it contains a specific prohibition of abortion. It calls upon doctors always to act in the best interests of their patients and to do them no harm. As I reviewed my position on abortion, I found that I was acting against all three of these principles.

(1) Abortion does not solve the patient's underlying problems and is not in her best interests:

It certainly is not in the best interests of my second patient, the baby. It was becoming increasingly apparent, as the years went by, as I continued to see these patients and follow them up, that abortion did not provide an adequate solution to the problems which so often lay beneath a request for the pregnancy to be terminated. In some situations the request arose out of the sheer inconvenience of being pregnant and, yes, it did provide an immediate answer to that problem, but not without cost. In the majority of cases, however, there were underlying socio-economic problems, marital dishar-mony and a whole host of fears, tensions and stress. In some circumstances, it was obvious that the girl had got herself pregnant simply because she wanted someone to love her and wanted someone of her own to love. Paradoxically this often led to an abortion request but was followed almost immediately by another pregnancy, despite adequate contraceptive advice. The next baby is kept.

It was apparent to me that I was not solving problems by destroying babies. It was also becoming increasingly clear that I was often adding to the patient's problems and doing her positive harm.

(2) Abortion can do positive harm:

(a) To the individual. While preparing for the Specialist Diploma some six years previously, I had undertaken a study of the short term complications of abortion in my Teaching Hospital. I found that, even in that 'centre of excellence', 33 per cent of patients had suffered a significant physical complication from the operation. One such complication — post operative infection — was noted in 10 per cent of patients at another such centre recently. I was finding it not at all uncommon to see patients present at the Infertility Clinic some years later who had had no problem getting pregnant before an abortion but were now infertile as a result of such infection. My survey did not include a look at the other long term complications, which have been under-reported, as the Department of Health and Social Security (DHSS) only requires doctors to report problems occurring in the first week after operation. Even these are not fully recorded as the patient will often return to a different hospital with the complications and a different doctor, who is under no obligation to report the complication even if he knows that it is due to an abortion. Guilt and depression are variable factors but again it is not uncommon to find a patient in tears at the birth of a subsequent baby as she remembers the baby it could have been and is not.

I was particularly interested in the effects of abortion on a subsequent pregnancy and had begun keeping careful records of all such patients who delivered in our Maternity Unit (I have now detailed some 550 such pregnancies). It was becoming apparent that such women had suffered harm. In particular, there was a far higher incidence of late miscarriage as a result of damage to the neck of the womb; bleeding late in the pregnancy and heavy bleeding often with retention of the afterbirth. It is always difficult to prove these associations as there can be so many other factors to take into account. It would take a far larger number of patients than I was seeing to do this but I was being convinced that harm had been done to these women and that as a result both they and the subsequent baby were suffering. My compassion for her initial predicament was causing me to act in a way which was not in her best interests and was causing her harm.

(b) To society. It was apparent to me that our abortion-orientated society was having an effect on my fellow doctors. It is difficult for the gynaecologist who has just come from the theatre where he has destroyed a 22 week old fetus, to fight with the same determination as he would previously have done to save the life of the 22 week old baby of the mother in the labour ward in premature labour. Infanticide was now being considered, and used, by paediatricians where a handicapped baby had escaped the attentions of the Obstetrician.

Nurses too were being affected by the Act and well qualified, caring individuals were now having to think twice about taking up a profession where a pro-life stand could mean problems during their training and limit their opportunities for advancement in their chosen career. The same could be said of junior doctors considering gynaecology as a speciality.

Society at large was also showing the effects of an abortion-orientated attitude, where life is cheap. Baby battering, child abuse, the sexual abuse of children and rape were all on the increase. The number of illegitimate births continued to soar despite easy abortion. Abortion was not solving the problems that the social reformers had promised us it would. Instead, it seemed to be increasing the problems of society.

I wondered too about the long term effects on the 'mothering' instincts of the up and coming generations of young women and the stability of family life. We may never know but I cannot see it bringing any benefit.

With these thoughts in mind I turned to the Scriptures. I was still prepared to defend my view of limited abortion where I could see no alternative but I was coming to see that even this position was both illogical and harmful. I was now to realise that it was also unscriptural.

(3) I could find no Scriptural warrant for abortion:
I could, in fact, find no mention of abortion — the deliberate termination of a pregnancy — in Scripture. The absence of specific mention of the subject would seem to reflect the fact that abortion was anathema to the ancient Jews. They saw the pregnant woman as being 'with child' from conception and abortion was therefore a special case of 'murder'. (The passage in Exodus 21 is discussed elsewhere in this volume.)

It was, however, possible to identify a number of important principles in Scripture which had a bearing on the problem of abortion. I found that Psalm 139 was a good place to start but that numerous other Scriptures amplified the verses of this Psalm.

(i) Man was created in the image of God and as such has a special place in creation and a special worth to God such that he was prepared to send his son to die for mankind.

Both the Psalmist (v.13) and Job (ch.10) talk about their creation by God within the womb. Clearly 'the process of embryonic growth is neither haphazard nor automatic, but a divine work of creative skill'.[1]

(ii) A new individual begins at conception.

I had a new 'revelation' of meaning of the numerous genealogies in Scripture where it tells us that someone 'begat' someone else. Surely this implies that the new person began at the time of the begetting and not at some later date! I also thought afresh about the implications of our Lord's conception which we speak of in the creeds when we say 'He was conceived by the Holy Spirit'. The Church has always recognised that conception was the point at which Jesus took on his humanity and the Scriptures set this forth as the normal experience of us all.

(iii) There is a continuity of life from conception.

The Psalmist refers to himself both prenatally and after birth by the same personal pronouns 'I' and 'me' — looking back to the past (v.1), to the present (vv.2–3) and the future (v.10), and again when thinking of his prenatal existence in verse 13. He knows no discontinuity. This point was brought home even more graphically when I learned that Luke uses the same Greek word to describe the unborn baby, the newborn child and the children brought to Jesus for his blessing. It was also interesting to read of Isaiah (44:2 and 49:1), Jeremiah (1:5) and Job (10:8 and 31:15) talking of their existence within the womb in personal terms. Job makes this point even clearer by contrasting his being still-born with his being 'as though I had not been', *ie* 'I', the real me, had been there within the womb. Paul also talks of his existence within the womb in his letter to the Galations (1:15). All these writers see God as personally involved in their prenatal existence and we also see God involved in the prenatal life of Esau, Jacob and Samson.

(iv) God has a relationship with the unborn.

D

The Psalmist expresses this 'I–you' relationship in almost every line of Psalm 139. Perhaps more important is his awareness of a 'you–me' relationship, a relationship established by Divine initiative before he could respond in conscious relationship to his God. It would seem that what makes us a person is not 'that we know God but that He knows us; not that we love God but that God has set His love upon us'.[2] This is seen in the relationships mentioned already which the Bible writers describe as existing between themselves and their God within the womb.

(v) Personality begins at conception.

It is not just a human life which begins at conception but a new person. All the facts I had so far uncovered implied that this was not just a 'something' which would become a 'someone' at some ill-defined later date. This was a *person* with whom God 'communed'. This was brought home again by re-reading the narrative regarding the incarnation of Jesus and the meeting of his mother with Elizabeth, the mother of John the Baptist, while both were pregnant. Elizabeth recognised the embryo Jesus as her 'Lord' (Luke 1:43) — this was no mere 'clump of cells' — and the fetal John was filled with the Holy Spirit and 'leaped for joy' in his mother's womb — an emotional response which implies the presence of personality.

(vi) God abhors 'the shedding of innocent blood'.

Elisha wept as he told Hazael what he would do to Israel, *ie* 'rip up their women with child' (2 Kings 8:12). Amos records God's judgement on Ammon for the same crime (1:13). Leviticus and Deuteronomy record God's abhorrence of those who sacrificed their children to the god Molech and later the prophets Isaiah, Jeremiah and Ezekiel condemn Israel for the same crime. In the light of what I had learned from Scripture and my appreciation of life as a continuum from conception to the grave, I was left asking: 'Is not modern man just sacrificing his children to another God — that of materialism'?

(vii) God has a special concern for the weak and the handicapped.

The Bible demonstrates that God requires care not killing. So much of antenatal screening is concerned with a 'seek and destroy' approach to the handicapped. The Old Testament goes as far as to curse him who exploits the handicapped (Lev. 19:14 and Deut. 27:18). Jesus spent much of his time bringing healing and wholeness to the diseased and the handicapped. The book of Revelation looks forward to the time when all such people will be made whole.

It seemed to me that to defend abortion meant that I had to say that there is such a human life as one who is *not* made in the image of God; one who is *not* of infinite value to him; one who is *not* known to God within the womb — for only then does this 'being' not demand the same reverence, value and protection that I would give to the rest of my fellow men. Could I say that there was such a being as a 'somebody' who is a 'nobody' in the sight of God?

Had I not been convinced already then my exploration of the scientific facts and philosophical arguments against abortion would have clinched the matter.

(4) Scientific and Philosophical reasoning support a pro-life stand:
Can we deny the fact that a new human life begins at conception? After all, this is a scientific fact and not a moral judgement. There is no other place along the path of human development at which one can draw the distinction between human and non-human. Fertilisation of a human egg by a human sperm will inevitably lead to the growth of a human being, given the right environment and proper nourishment. I am glad to see that even the pro-abortionist has now switched his line of attack and no longer talks of a 'clump of cells'. He has however coined a new pseudo-scientific term which allows his conscience to rest easy as he advocates experiments on the 'pre embryo'. One of my colleagues jokingly asked if the term could be applied to a lustful thought!

The suggestion has been made that the more appropriate point to recognise as the beginning of the new being is his/her implantation within the womb. It has also been said that the new being has only the *potential* for true human life and that we should recognise that his/her worth increases as he/she grows to maturity within the womb and is not of equal value with the rest of us. Biblically, we have seen this to be a fallacy. Philosophically much the same can be said. I can never become what I have not been from the beginning of my existence. 'I' was 'I' from conception, or 'I' do not exist at all. I can never say that I was a sperm or an egg, but I can say that I was an embryo or a fetus. There is no point of my existence when I can say that at that point I actually was, but before that I did not exist other than at the point of my conception, *ie* at the fertilisation of my mother's egg by my father's sperm. I also believe that there is no such person as a 'potential human being'; it is an illogicality, there are only human beings with potential. Personhood is not something that I achieve when I reach a certain size or when it is proven that I am physically perfect or have a certain IQ. Personhood is not a matter of my achievement. It is something bestowed upon me by my Creator when he creates me in his image.

During the time of my reflections, the techniques of ultrasound and fetoscopy have been refined. These scientific marvels allow the obstetrician, and often the mother, to have a window into the womb. When one has seen the baby's heart beating at six weeks from conception and watched his growing features during the early weeks of pregnancy, one cannot deny the humanity of this individual. It seems little realised that the baby is fully formed by the twelfth week from conception and that all he/she has to do from that point is to develop to a point where he can survive, still with mother's help, outside the womb. Implantation, like delivery, is not the start of life, it is simply a change of environment for this new individual.

There is much going on within the womb beside the physical development of the baby. A recent publication, entitled *The Secret Life of the Unborn Child*, has brought together a vast amount of research which has been done in this area and shows very clearly that the baby is increasingly aware of his environment as he/she develops within the womb and is responding to various stimuli and influences. It throws a very interesting light on the concepts of personhood and the biblical writers' view of life before birth.

It is a sad reflection on our society that the womb, which should be a place of safety and security, has been described as the place where one is most likely to be the victim of violence in our all too violent world. It is also said that a civilisation will be judged by its treatment of its weakest members. What will future generations say of a society which talked of 'preventing handicap' by destroying the evidence rather than seeking its causes and truly preventing its occurence.

How then do I justify my decision not to perform abortions?

(1) Because I think it does positive harm to my patients:
It has been rightly said that if the harm done to patients by abortion had been attributed to any drug, it would have been immediately withdrawn from the market. It is a schizophrenic society which ignores these facts and allows it.

(2) I believe that I am dealing with two patients not one:
There is no other situation in medicine where one would consider the destruction of a patient as being in his/her best interests or where it is allowable to alleviate the suffering of another patient. I do not think the day is far off when I will no longer be able to make that statement. Abortion has already opened the gate to infanticide and will open the floodgate of euthanasia before long, if we are not careful to prevent it.

My compassion for the patient sitting in front of me blinded my eyes to the presence of the baby for many years. I believe now that I misunderstood the true meaning of compassion. It can only operate effectively within the framework of God's law and only then will the ultimate worth of the individual be recognised and his/her best interests be upheld.

(3) I believe that abortion is wrong in God's sight:
It will be clear by now that I believe that God has set down a framework within which we can operate and given us the necessary principles to guide our actions. I do not believe that I can see it as 'the lesser of two evils'; that is

not the way my God operates. It is no good my saying that God does not understand the problems of modern day society — he does. I cannot bend the rules to suit my patient's needs or to keep myself in everyone's good books. I believe that my Lord does have an answer to the problems that my patients face and it is for me to help them find those answers without introducing abortion as an option.

(4) I believe that there is a better way:
In saying all this, I am aware that the patient may not see it that way and may well not accept my advice, but that is true in other spheres of medicine too. I need to be willing to show God's love in action and to reach out with viable and relevant alternatives and suggestions. I cannot say 'no' to abortion and walk away from the problems in the same way as I could say 'yes' and then wash my hands after the operation and walk away from them. Saying 'no' involves me in helping the patient in her dilemma and the problems she faces. I need the help of a caring Christian community in doing this. It may mean my opening my home and taking her in. It could involve the sacrifice of time, money, privacy and other things that I hold dear, but that is what my Lord demands of me and I must be willing to respond to him. It is far easier to say 'yes' to the abortion.

God's way will bring love where there is hate; hope where there is despair; order where there is chaos; wholeness and healing where there is disease and life and joy instead of death and guilt.

Some of the practical difficulties and dilemmas of a pro-life stand

(1) Should I refuse to see patients requesting abortion?
No. It is part of my calling to provide a caring service for all patients who come to see me and I will always do that which I think is best for them. In actual fact, such patients or their GPs, will often decide for themselves that they do not wish to see a doctor who will not carry out abortions. Until that happens the pro-life doctor should continue to see them. Such patients still need a Christian counsellor and to experience Christian caring. It is not unusual to find that a caring approach and a reasoned explanation of all that abortion entails and the alternatives available, will cause some to think again and change their minds. Some just do not know what facilities can be offered to help them in their predicament.

(2) What about the GP who opposes abortion — should he see and refer such patients?
The GP is under no obligation to refer such patients. Again, I think he should continue to see those who come to him. As it becomes known that he does not

sanction abortion, fewer will come. It will have an effect on his practice and he will suffer in other ways. There will always be those who accuse him of showing a lack of love and compassion.

I believe however that God is true to his word when he says, 'those who honour me I will honour' (1 Sam.2:30). He proved himself to the Israeli midwives who refused to obey the instructions of Pharaoh to kill the Israeli boys and he will continue to keep his promise and bless those who keep his law rather than the law of men. I think the GP will also find that his/her patients will appreciate the obvious love and concern that he/she shows as he/she shares in their heartache.

(3) What about neonatal screening?

We are often assured that it is best to eliminate the 'defective' fetus. We are assured that this is in the best interests of the mother, society and the infant itself, whose life will not be worth living. Thus it is important to develop neonatal screening services.

We need to distinguish between those tests which are done to identify a condition so that it can be treated within the womb and thereby save the life of the baby, and those done with the object of identifying a handicapped baby so that it can be destroyed. The former we should support. The latter is often promoted as a means of 'preventing' handicap. We need to appreciate that the handicap has already occurred and we are about to destroy the evidence by killing the affected baby.

We have seen something of God's concern for the weak, the defenceless and the handicapped. We cannot say that it is in accord with his will to kill them. We do not have the right, either, to say that another's life is not worth living. Yes, it will mean problems for the family. It will put a strain on a marriage. None of us would wish to be born handicapped, but killing is not the answer. Unfortunately, in a society which makes a God of economic efficiency, it is more 'cost effective' to abort the handicapped than to provide the facilities which will enable them to develop their full potential. Such a situation also means that the funds will never be made available to promote research which will effectively prevent such handicap. We need to consider also what such an attitude says to those already born and suffering handicap — what insecurity they must feel in such a society.

(4) Would I abort a handicapped baby?

I have carried out abortion in certain cases of severe handicap where I was convinced that the baby would not survive the pregnancy and where to let the pregnancy continue would have added significantly to the risks of the pregnancy and the delivery of the mother.

I am not convinced now of the rightness of that course of action. It will always be difficult to know where to draw the line in advocating such an approach but there is another more important consideration. This is usually a much wanted baby. In suggesting that the pregnancy be terminated I am involving the mother in the decision to destroy wilfully her baby and she knows that fact. It has been clearly shown that such women are especially likely to suffer from guilt and depression in later years and they need very careful counsel and support.

I wonder whether it is not better to counsel the mother to continue with the pregnancy and let 'nature take its course'. I certainly now present that as an option, providing as I have said, that it does not increase the risks to her life to do so. She will then know that she has given her baby every chance in life and not have to suffer the guilt of participating in his/her death.

(5) How do I respond to the women who say it is their right to decide what happens to their bodies?

I would point out that the 1967 Abortion Act gives no one any rights. It simply defines certain situations in which abortion is permissible without involving any of the parties in a criminal offence. Such an action can only be decided upon by two doctors deciding 'in good faith' that the woman's problems fall within the allowable conditions of the Act:

1 Subject to the provisions of this section, a person shall not be guilty of an offence under the law relating to abortion when a pregnancy is terminated by a registered medical practitioner if two registered medical practitioners are of the opinion, formed in good faith —
(a) that the continuance of the pregnancy would involve risk to the life of the pregnant woman, or of injury to the physical or mental of the pregnant woman or any existing children of her family, greater than if the pregnancy were terminated; or
(b) that there is a substantial risk that if the child were born it would suffer from such physical or mental abnormalities as to be seriously handicapped.
2 In determining whether the continuance of a pregnancy would involve such risk of injury to health as is mentioned in paragraph (a) of subsection 1 of this section, account may be taken of the pregnant woman's actual or reasonably foreseeable environment.

I would also point out that we are not simply talking about her body but that of an entirely separate individual. I think the advent of 'test-tube babies' has put an end to this myth. We are talking about a separate individual who can survive for a while outside his/her mother's womb in those early days of pregnancy but who does need her if he/she is to grow to maturity. A statement which is equally true of the newborn baby.

(6)What alternatives can I offer?

It is important to have relevant and practical advice to offer. It is even more important to be able to offer practical help. My first action was to join the organisation LIFE which I knew was able to offer accommodation to those who needed it and was also involved in the other important areas of eduation and political action. There were no Christian organisations involved in these matters at that time.

A year ago we were able to start opening our own home to such women in need. At the same time Care Trust began to look for a 1000 Christian homes which would offer refuge to these and other folk in need. We joined the scheme and my wife is now involved in co-ordinating the work in our region of the country. We have had two pregnant girls staying with us during the year, from very different backgrounds. Both have had their babies. One opted for adoption and the other has kept her baby. We, and the local church, were very much involved with them throughout their pregnancies. The Church was able to show its love in very practical ways when it came to helping the second girl and her fiancée set up home. She was not a Christian but she certainly saw and appreciated the love of Christ in action. We all grew in stature through that experience.

In Conclusion

I do not see that abortion can be an option either for the Christian doctor or for the pregnant Christian woman. God has laid down a very clear framework in his word within which we must live and work. He does understand our modern culture and its problems, he created us. He does know what is best for us. Killing the defenceless unborn is not part of his plan for his creation.

This means there must be a change of attitude within his Church towards the woman who is pregnant out of wedlock. We took in one of the girls because the Church would literally have excommunicated her family had they known of the pregnancy. I have recently been counselling a family who forced their daughter to undergo an abortion because they could not face the 'disgrace' and condemnation that they would feel within their 'Church'. They now bitterly regret their action as they face the grief of their daughter who knows she has 'murdered' her baby. Only Jesus can bring forgiveness and peace to that family and they are beginning to experience his healing.

What must Christ think of that Church? Someone has aptly commented that if all the people in the Church who had ever entertained a lustful thought were to develop swollen tummies, there would be a lot of embarrassed faces in the pews. Jesus said that the thought is as bad as the action. In both cases it is the sin which is condemned, not the sinner. It is far easier to get an abortion done quietly out of the glare of publicity than to face the embarrassed looks and spoken or unspoken condemnation of our 'brothers and sisters' in Christ, Such attitudes must change if we are to help such folk obey the will of Christ for them and their babies. Okay, so they have done wrong, but 'let him who is without sin cast the first stone'. Only then will many feel able to continue with their pregnancies, and only then can we expect society's attitude to change and we will begin to see an end to the slaughter of the innocent.

It also means that we must be prepared for the cost of showing that we really care. The family of God does have the means to provide an alternative but are we prepared for the sacrifice involved? It will not be an answer which is acceptable to all or even most but there are those who are crying out for us to show that we care, that we understand and that we are willing to help them in their need. God will help us do that and he will bless us in the doing of his will.

Notes to Paper 7

1   Dr Bernard Nathanson, see for instance, N Bernard, MD, with Richard Ostling, *Aborting America* (Doubleday, New York, 1979). Dr Nathanson was responsible for the production of the film, *The Silent Scream*, which presents an ultrasound record of an abortion taking place.
2   I K Grigor, *Responses to Warnock, A Review: Ethics and Medicine* (1986), 2:2, pp 25–31.

Recommended Reading

Nigel de Cameron and Pamela Sims, *Abortion — the Crisis in Morals and Medicine* (Inter-Varsity Press).
Schaeffer and Koop, *Whatever Happened to the Human Race?* (Marshall, Morgan and Scott, London).
John Stott, *Issues Facing Christians Today* (Marshalls), p 287 — reference 1; p 288 — reference 2.

8

Issues Facing the Medical Profession

There is nothing remotely pleasant about abortion: it is difficult and painful (at least in a psychological sense) for the woman or girl, it is a matter of anxiety and guilt for her partner (unless he is totally unfeeling), it is a source of grief and difficulty for the wider families involved, and it is a complex and challenging issue for all who are called upon to counsel and to undertake the procedure. It is an issue in which doctors (gynaecologists, general practitioners, psychiatrists and clinic medical officers) are obliged to become involved and to have a view, either as active participants or as providers of counsel, advice, assessment and referral.

Historically doctors, until the middle of this century, have been generally opposed to the practice of abortion. It is specifically prohibited in the Hippocratic Oath, and in England it became a statutory offence at the beginning of the nineteenth century — although in Scotland abortion was not constrained by any specific legislation until 1967. It is not clear whether this historical medical objection was based on ethical and moral considerations or on the very real dangers of abortion in the pre-antibiotic era. What is clear is that it was the appalling effects of illegal or 'back street' abortions in terms of both morbidity and mortality which prompted the 1967 legislation.

The provisions of this Act are that an abortion performed by a registered medical practitioner is legal:

1 Subject to the provisions of this section, a person shall not be guilty of an offence under the law relating to abortion when a pregnancy is terminated by a registered medical practitioner if two registered medical practitioners are of the opinion, formed in good faith —

(a) that the continuance of the pregnancy would involve risk to the life of the pregnant woman, or of injury to the physical or mental health of the pregnant woman or any existing children of her family, greater than if the pregnancy were terminated; or

(b) that there is a substantial risk that if the child were born it would suffer from such physical or mental abnormalities as to be seriously handicapped.

2 In determining whether the continuance of a pregnancy would involve such risk of injury to health as is mentioned in paragraph (a) of subsection 1 of this section, account may be taken of the pregnant woman's actual or reasonably foreseeable environment.

Why has the medical profession in this country (certainly not all the profession, but a substantial majority) moved from the position of supporting the absolute prohibition enshrined in the Hippocratic Oath to accepting the terms of the 1967 Act? There are probably three main reasons: first, doctors had been faced with the sometimes appalling and occasionally fatal results of the late effects of illegal or 'back street' abortions, both in terms of physical and of psychological suffering. Second, advances in gynaecological, medical and anaesthetic technology has made therapeutic terminations of pregnancy both safer and simpler. Third, advances in understanding about embryology has helped to clarify the biological debate.

It may be said in parenthesis that (contrary to popular belief) doctors in the United Kingdom do not formally swear the Hippocratic Oath; indeed it is only in the Scottish medical schools that any form of oath is sworn at graduation — based generally on the spirit of the Hippocratic Oath but omitting long since any references either to abortion or to 'cutting for stone'.

Illegal Pregnancy Termination

There is ample evidence that illegal 'do-it-yourself' or 'back street' abortions were common before 1968; the numbers could not of course be known with any degree of accuracy as the activity was technically illegal and therefore rarely reported, but it has been estimated that at least 20 000 and possibly as many as 100 000 illegal abortions were carried out annually in the United Kingdom.

Many doctors practising at that time will recollect women involved in non-medical abortions who were, as a result, ill with sepsis or suffering after haemorrhage, and who were sometimes made subsequently sterile, often guilty, anxious or depressed, some of them to this day bearing physical or psychological scars.

Undoubtedly some women were able to obtain termination of pregnancy under medical supervision if they were able to pay for private treatment, particularly after the Bourne case in England in 1938 when the judge ruled that it was lawful to terminate a pregnancy not only to save a woman's life but also if 'the continuation of the pregnancy would make the woman a physical or mental wreck'. The majority of women however had either to carry an unwanted pregnancy to term or subject themselves to dangerous, squalid and guilt-ridden procedures.

Advances in Technology

The major complications of termination of pregnancy were blood loss and infection. Newer methods (such as suction aspiration and the use of prostaglandins) minimise the risks, and the more ready availability of blood transfusion and antibiotics lessen the dangers still further. Advances in anaesthesia have been less dramatically apparent but are nonetheless real and significantly reduce the hazards of all operative procedures.

Embryology

In the continuing debate about abortion it is important that embryology terms are carefully defined. It is unnecessarily distressing and scientifically inaccurate to describe termination of pregnancy at an early stage as the 'killing of babies' or 'tearing children from their mothers' wombs'.

From the moment of fertilisation the fused ovum and sperm becomes a *conceptus* which may or may not implant in the womb. This conceptus on implantation becomes an embryo with potential to develop into a fetus — a term often used loosely, but defined as 'the young animal in the womb after its parts are distinctly formed' (in the human species this is after the end of the second month). The fetus continues to develop to become at birth an infant, baby or child. This developing organism in all its stages up to the severance of the umbilical cord is totally dependent on a nutritional support system formed from the maternal circulation — there is no sense in which it can be described as 'independent'.

The Christian Perspective

It is sometimes implied that the question of abortion poses greater moral and ethical dilemmas for the doctor who is a practising Christian than for a doctor of other faiths or of none. This is not necessarily true, as all doctors subscribe, or attempt to subscribe to some ethical code, and all are faced — at least to some degree — with the ethical implications of their decisions.

The question of abortion, like that of (for instance) nuclear weapons, presents moral dilemmas for which Scripture offers no direct guidance. Some theologians maintain that the moral rights of the developing conceptus, embryo and fetus are equal to the moral rights of a baby, child or adult. Other theologians (possibly a majority, at least in the Protestant Churches) would see a gradation of moral rights, and this would be the stance adopted by Christian doctors who are not totally opposed to abortion and see it as a sometimes necessary evil, but one which is, in the balance of all factors, a lesser evil than a 'back street' abortion or the birth of an unwanted, unloved and resented child.

Much of the argument centres on the problems of defining the beginning, the status and the meaning of 'life'. The fertilised ovum or conceptus is in a certain sense alive, genetically unique and human — but only in the sense that a sperm or an unfertilised ovum is likewise alive, unique and human. There is a substantial natural wastage of conceptuses and embryos — variously estimated at between 20 per cent and in excess of 50 per cent of all conceptions. Such spontaneous abortions may cause disappointment or even grief, but the loss and the sense of loss is not of the same order as a still-birth or neonatal death, and in a substantial proportion of miscarriages they may not even be recognised.

Biologically there is a case for claiming that an individual life begins at the moment of fertilisation, but even in a biological sense it is a conditional, even a parasitic life, and in no sense an independent one.

The central theological debate revolves around the question of personality or soul. It is at the very least debatable that a developing cluster of cells, organising into tissues, systems and organs could be said to have a personality or soul. Scripture is silent on the point. Some theologians call upon the incarnation in their support, but this is surely to confuse theology and biology; the incarnation was a unique, tremendous Divine event; procreation is a common recurring biological activity.

Life is more than a concatenation of molecules. In religious terms life is a matter of relationships, and pre-eminently in Christianity a matter of love. A baby at birth is an object of love in a clear and obvious sense; a developing embryo is not. This is not to say that the developing embryo must not be accorded respect and consideration for its potential to become a person, soul or human being, it is merely to indicate that its moral rights can legitimately be considered to be of a different order.

The historical debate about the beginning of life in the theological sense, as opposed to the strictly cellular one, has ancient antecedents. Thomas Aquinas followed Aristotle in believing that 'ensoulment' occurred for boys at 40 days and for girls at 90 days, showing a degree of precision and discrimination which would today be unlikely to be found acceptable. The question is not one which science can solve — human nature is a more complex matter than the sum of all the genes. The fertilised ovum is a physical basis for a person, it is not in itself a person; the embryo is a potential person arising from the fusion of two gametes — the resulting fetus cannot and should not be considered out of the context into which it might be born. That context is most immediately the family. The pivot of the family is the woman in whose womb that embryo is implanted — the mother. Even those most vehemently opposed to the practice of abortion concede that the mother at least has moral rights of a different order to those of the embryo when it is accepted that extreme danger to the life of the mother may be a legitimate ground for termination of pregnancy.

The Issues Facing the Medical Profession

Termination of pregnancy is legal within the constraints noted above.

Whether it is desirable is often debatable. A doctor, and particularly a general practitioner, faced with a request for termination has a duty both to counsel the patient and to attempt to ensure necessary services and support. Counselling is not, as it is sometimes thought, a process of direction; it is a method of informing the woman of the choices and options open to her and enabling her to come to a decision with as much information as possible about the course of action she wishes to pursue. This is not an easy task as the issues are invariably complex and the context is inevitably one of distress and guilt.

Abortion 'on demand' is not an option — were it so the practitioner could hardly be said to be acting in good faith with regard to the criteria laid down in the Act. It is undeniable that the criteria are widely drawn and their interpretation open to considerable latitude. It is the practitioner's responsibility to ensure that adequate consideration is given to the likely effects, as far as they can be assessed, both of a possible termination and of a possible continuation of the pregnancy on all the parties involved.

General practitioners are trained to formulate their diagnoses by taking into consideration physical, psychological and social factors: it is this triad of factors which has to be explored in abortion counselling. Doctors who have a conscientious objection to abortion have an ethical obligation, if consulted by a woman or girl contemplating termination of pregnancy, to refer the patient to a colleague. A practitioner who does not have such a conscientious objection but who feels after adequate discussion and counselling that he cannot support a recommendation for termination (and the patient after such counselling persists with the request) has a similar obligation to refer the patient, with a statement of his reasons for declining to make the recommendation.

For the doctor, the crucial issues involved in counselling are issues of relationship: the relationship of the patient with the child which might be born as the result of the conception; the relationship of the patient and the father of the future child; the relationship of the patient with her own parents, with other caring agencies including the possibilities of adoption and of care during and after the pregnancy whether proceeded with or not. Some of these are existing relationships and other estimates of possible future relationships — at best subjective judgements but often most adequately explored by a professional with knowledge of the family, social and cultural background — a role most likely to be filled by a general practitioner, especially if he has the help of health visitors and/or social workers.

In a perfect world all pregnancies would be wanted and all children conceived in love; some, alas, are conceived in 'carelessness, fecklessness, ignorance, drunkenness, witlessness, gullibility, violence or rape'. To abort a potential human life is rarely if ever a positive good, but it may be the lesser of a number of evils. Within both the Hippocratic ethic and the imperative of

Christian concern, while approval may or may not be elicited, the obligation of care remains.

Response to Peter J Armon

Dr Armon's thoughtful, sincere and at times moving paper commands respect, but, perhaps not surprisingly, it does not command agreement. Not surprisingly because the central issue is a theological and ethical one and where eminent theologians and recognised experts in the field of medical ethics fail to agree, it is only to be expected that medical practitioners will sincerely hold views reflecting the same division of opinion and interpretation.

So much revolves around the definition of 'life'. The term 'pro-life' used by those who oppose abortion tends to beg the fundamental question, and its implication that those who hold different views are 'anti-life' can be objectionable. Equally difficult are the considerations that the termination of pregnancy can in certain circumstances be a lesser evil than a 'back street' abortion, or that the continuation of an unwanted pregnancy should not be said to be 'pro-abortionist'. I would also take issue with the phrase 'Christian GP' being used to imply a GP who 'will not sanction abortion'. There are GPs of all faiths and of none, who disapprove of abortion as well as those of all faiths and of none (but certainly including professing Christians) who are prepared in given circumstances to 'sanction' abortion.

The meaning of the concept of man made in the image of God is surely a spiritual one; the concept of 'life' beginning at conception is purely a biological one.

The genealogy of our Lord in the first chapter of Matthew ends with Joseph the husband of Mary: there are interesting implications here if we wish to consider the genetic uniqueness of the man Jesus alongside the credal statement, 'conceived by the Holy Ghost'. This is deep theological water indeed, but not, in my view, relevant to the debate about the development of the human soul or personality — or even of the biological organism. Luke's description of the encounter between Elizabeth and Mary is one of beautiful symbolism (and gives us the wonderful poetry of the Magnificat in Luke 1:46–55) but it is unlikely that it is meant to be taken as a literal and accurate account of events. Even if it is, the relationship described must surely be taken to be a reflection of the divinity of Jesus rather than his humanity, and therefore unhelpful in deciding the question of the human soul or human personality.

I would certainly agree with Dr Armon's observation that Scripture teaches us nothing directly about abortion. Clearly we have to differ in our interpretations of what Scripture does teach us about human life and the obligation of love. I fully accept an obligation to love those with whom we relate; I do not accept that we can relate to the early developing embryo, although we may respect its potential to become a fully human personality.

112

Dr Armon's practical involvement in the care of girls with unwanted pregnancies with its possibly sacrificial involvement in his own family's life is in many ways admirable and commendable. His sincere belief that his stance and his actions reflect the will of God has to be respected, but the will of God may not always be easily discerned. Are spontaneous miscarriages, infertility or cerebral palsy the will of God? Is it the will of God that pregnancy must continue after rape, after thoughtless, feckless coition with a schoolgirl barely past puberty, or after contraceptive failure in a pre-menopausal mother already burdened by major family responsibilities? God moves in a mysterious way and his will may be reflected in unattractive solutions which are at best sincere attempts to recognise the complexities of human relationships.

Love is undoubtedly the moral imperative, but love is unconditional and cannot be bound by rules or dogma. It is clear that on the subject of abortion there is not one Christian view but several. The debate will not cease and commited Christians will continue to disagree, but, with faith and hope, love will abide.

Response to J J C Cormack

Dr Cormack states that, 'There is nothing remotely pleasant about abortion' (p 106), and 'to abort ... is rarely, if ever, a positive good' (p 110). We are agreed on these points, but he goes on to say that it 'may be the lesser of a number of evils' (p 110). I cannot see evil as an option for the Christian. I would agree, as far as the patient is concerned, that whatever one's attitude, 'the obligation for care remains' (p 111).

Dr Cormack suggests three reasons why the attitude of the medical profession has changed in the years since 1967. I will look at these. I think, however, that one of the main reasons why both the public and the profession accept the present situation is the growing feeling that what the Law allows is necessarily morally right.

Illegal pregnancy termination

There is no factual evidence to support the statement that 'possibly as many as 100 000 abortions were carried out annually' (p 107), prior to 1967. If there were, then the maternal mortality statistics suggest that the back street abortionist was doing a far better job than the NHS in the years immediately following the Act.

I would also point out that I still see patients 'ill with sepsis or suffering after haemorrhage, and who were sometimes made subsequently sterile and often guilty and depressed' (p 107) following legal termination.

I do not think there ever would be a return to the 'appalling effects of ... back street abortions' (p 107) if the 1967 Act were repealed. The advent of the antibiotic era and the more sophisticated methods of abortion available, even the possibility of the DIY kit, would see to that.

Advances in Technology

There have certainly been advances in the techniques of surgery and anaesthesia but complications still occur. In the light of the 170 000 abortions now done annually, this means a considerable number of women harmed by the complications that I have described.

Embryology

It is advances in understanding in this realm which has caused many doctors to turn against abortion. Dr Nathanson, America's leading abortionist, gives this as his primary reason for a change of mind. Now he is a leading campaigner against abortion.

Dr Cormack uses the term 'potential person' and uses this and the dependency of the embryo as reasons for its lesser worth. I would re-emphasise that there is no such creature as a 'potential person'. Scientifically, philosophically and spiritually, there can only be a person with potential and that person exists from conception. I would also point out that the newborn baby is still equally as dependent on his/her mother for nurture as it was prior to the severance of the cord.

Examining Some of Dr Cormack's Other Points:
I think my paper has already shown that far from the Scriptures offering 'no direct guidance' on this issue, a very clear framework is laid down within which we can approach the issue of abortion.

I hope that I have shown that there is ample evidence from within Scripture and without, that a new human person begins his life at conception. Surely this individual is utterly different in his/her being 'alive, unique and human' as compared to an egg or sperm!

It has been shown recently that the majority of Churches in this country do not support the theory of the gradually developing worth of the embryo.

I would strongly dispute the statement that the sense of loss following a spontaneous abortion is not of the same order as that following a still-birth. The many miscarriage support groups that have sprung up around the country bear eloquent testimony to the fact that doctors do not appreciate this fact. They should perhaps also warn us of problems that women having abortions are not always so openly expressing.

I agree that 'life is a matter of relationships' and have sought to show that it is the relationship which God has already established with the embryo in the womb which makes him/her a unique individual of infinite worth to the Creator.

I agree whole-heartedly that every doctor has the obligation to provide the best possible care for all of his patients whether or not he takes a pro-life or abortionist stance. I do not agree that he is under any obligation to refer a patient for a procedure which he does not feel is in her best interest and may do her positive harm and which is certainly not in the best interest of his second patient — the baby.

9

Reflections on whether Abortion is a Just and Loving Solution to Problems in Pregnancy

By a Counsellor who also happens to be a Christian

People who oppose abortion do not have to be Christian or indeed have any religious faith. It is enough to believe in the dignity and equal value of all human life and to refuse to accept deliberate and direct killing of innocent and defenceless people as a just solution to any problem, however desperate.

Abortion kills another human being. All the medical and biological evidence points to the fact that human life begins at fertilisation. Implantation by the human embryo in the womb, quickening, viability, birth, are incidents in human life, not the beginning of it. This is factual knowledge, not 'belief' or guesswork.

The Christian has additional reasons for opposing abortion. The central doctrine of Christianity is that God himself became a man 'for us men and for our salvation'. The Gospel records and the creeds make it clear that this humanity began at conception, not at birth or at any other stage in pregnancy. The second person of the Blessed Trinity himself became a zygote, an embryo, a fetus in the womb of his mother.

The incarnation took place at conception (Matt.1:20): very God and very man was with us, then and there. And if our Lord's personal life as a human being began at conception, so must ours. Thus Christians have theological as well as scientific grounds for asserting that human life begins at conception.

Human life must be of quite exceptional importance if God himself was prepared to assume it. The Bible establishes that we are all made in the image and likeness of God (Gen 1:26–28; 2:7) and that this is the basis of man's dignity and worth.

To the Christian therefore the unborn child is, or should be realised as being, his or her brother or sister in the womb. This does not mean that the Christian should be concerned only with the unborn child. There should be as much concern for the pregnant woman or girl as with her baby. Both are equally precious and unique, and need help and care in order for the pregnancy to continue. The woman facing the problems and difficulties of an

116

unwanted pregnancy is a sister too, and needs and deserves every possible help in overcoming her problems without recourse to abortion. The Christian response to problems in pregnancy should be loving and positive, and it should acknowledge the dignity and value of both lives, the mother's and the unborn child's.

It is important here to emphasise that the counselling provided by LIFE, the organisation with which I am directly involved, does not involve religious discussion, and the personal beliefs of the counsellor are held carefully in check. The same can be said of other pro-life organisations engaged in the field of counselling. Counsellors are motivated simply by their belief in the value of human life. The task facing the counsellor is to help an individual clarify the critical issues facing her towards reaching a decision. This process, of its nature, could in fact be impeded by the inappropriate insertion of the counsellor's personal beliefs. The counsellor is trained to avoid this.

Anyone who counsels women and girls with the problem of an unwanted pregnancy must examine their own motives and try to free themselves of any desire to 'push' a woman towards the counsellor's own view. It would seem to me then that anyone who stands to gain financially by the women's decision is compromised. It is unrealistic to expect the employees of abortion-providing agencies or advice bureaux linked to abortion clinics to give genuine pregnancy counselling. They should be called abortion advisers and their role be seen for what it is: part of the growing and profitable abortion industry. For some reason it is considered to be in bad taste to point out the obvious: there is a lot of money to be made in providing women with abortions, whether in the private sector, or on the National Health Service where the aborting doctor gets a capitation fee for each abortion over and above his or her NHS salary. Counsellors employed in the private sector in particular must, however hard they deny it, be conscious that they are paid from the profits of abortion and their advice in most circumstances must be coloured by that knowledge. These counsellors who believe that abortion is right, cannot consider that the life of the unborn child is as important as the happiness of the mother who does not want to be pregnant. They would claim that for them the overriding concern is with the woman and her problems, and arranging a quick, easy and legal way out of them.

The motives of pregnancy counsellors who do not agree with abortion are more complicated. Generally, counsellors with pro-life organisations are trained, but unpaid, volunteers, so there is no financial motive and no big business empire to support. They have two apparently contradictory beliefs. The first is that the unborn child is a unique human being from the moment of fertilisation onwards and as such should not be killed at any time from fertilisation to birth (or after). They are also moved by the fact that the unborn child is unseen and unheard and has no means of defending his/herself or of putting up a case for survival. So a counsellor working in an organisation such as LIFE is partly an advocate for the life of the unborn child, usually finding that no one else advising the mother is so concerned.

The second belief of LIFE counsellors is that women should have full equality and dignity accorded to them and should be helped through a difficult situation — such as an unplanned pregnancy — to the solution that is going to be best for the woman herself not only in the immediate future but in the long term as well. All LIFE counsellors are women.

These two beliefs are, ideally, held with equal conviction: the humanity and equal value of the unborn child, and the dignity and need for help of the mother. These beliefs meet and mingle in a third conviction: that abortion is never a just, loving and, in the long term especially, efficient response to a woman's problems.

The Lesser of Two Evils?

Some people, including some Christians, who support abortion do so because they see it as the lesser of two evils. The birth of a child is reckoned, in some circumstances, to be such an evil or to bring such tragic problems with it that the death of the child is preferable. Pro-life Christians would say that such thinking is a counsel of despair, ignoring not only God's creative powers but also his power to help and comfort those in need. No human problem can justly be solved by the direct and deliberate killing of another, with no other purpose than to kill someone whose existence poses problems. If we extended our society's acceptance of killing as a solution to social problems we would eliminate many people who, unlike the unborn child, have proved themselves to be destructive members of society.

Our society takes advantage of the very helplessness of the innocent unborn to inflict a 'solution' that it has consciously, and in my view, rightly rejected for criminals. There is a double standard here that Christians should expose, but which, alas, affects those Christians who support abortion.

There is also the argument for freedom of choice. People who support and counsel for abortion often do so because they want to help women and abortion has been skilfully marketed as an essential ingredient in women's struggle for greater equality with men, and for more control over their own lives. Leaving aside the wilder extremes of pro-abortion campaigners who will not be content until free abortion is mandatorily available on demand up to birth, there are people uneasy about 'too much' abortion but who want abortion to be freely available when needed. Others think that one's personal opposition to abortion should not spill over into attempting to deny others the benefits of the lesser of two evils.

It is said that the greater evil is to have to continue the pregnancy, give birth to an unwanted child, to have to make a hard decision whether or not to keep the child, risk losing job, boyfriend, lover, ruin marriage, hurt parents, or for any other reasons. The assumption is always that abortion *for the woman* brings unmitigated relief and freedom from all these problems, and so, despite the inevitable killing of the child, abortion is, for those who are more concerned with women than unborn babies, the best solution, and should be made available as a freely chosen option.

Until recently, sexual liberty was reckoned to bring considerable benefits to women as well as men. Abortion is an essential ingredient because there are no completely effective methods of preventing conception, and the aim of sexual liberty is that sexual enjoyment should be distinct from procreation. From the early 1960s the message has been promoted hard from every kind of platform and media outlet that sex is a happy-making pastime in itself and only causes misery and problems when it results in unwanted conception. In order for women to have the same sexual freedom as men, abortion is essential, otherwise a woman is 'punished' by pregnancy for her freedom.

A woman's body is therefore, with contraception backed up by easy abortion, permanently available for contraception-free sexual intercourse. This could be sexual freedom for women. Or it could be sexual enslavement. Slogans abound — 'It's my body, my choice/a women's right to choose' — that link abortion and sexual and indeed female liberation indissolubly. The assumption is that women *choose* to have sexual liberty and then *choose* whether or not to have abortions.

It is worth examining exactly how much free choice women have. There are no statistics available to grade how freely the 2 500 000 women who have had abortions made their choice. But after 16 years of pro-life pregnancy counselling my informed guess is that very few women actively and freely choose abortion. They have abortions in many cases because they are under implicit or explicit pressures to do so. In saying that I am not saying that those women were weak willed, or cowardly or immature in submitting to such pressure. But I am saying that when one is panic stricken and frightened, in a situation not of one's deliberate choosing, such as being unwantedly pregnant, much will turn upon the advice and support from those most intimately involved.

And that is where the 'freedom to choose' becomes almost laughably lacking. Anyone who promotes abortion in the name of freedom for women should stop for a moment and work out exactly who benefits. Is it the pregnant girl under 16 — or is it her parents who, if she has an abortion, will not have to cope with her interrupted schooling, face neighbours' and relations' curiosity and criticism, become grandparents before their time? Is it the older single girl, or her boyfriend, who will not have to support her financially or emotionally or feel guilty if he doesn't? Is it the married woman or her husband? For the truth is that abortion gets a lot of people off a hook, and the reactions of most of those around the young girl affected will be to urge her to have an abortion, or threaten her, if she does not. Let us look in detail at some typical examples.

The parents of an under age girl who may or may not be surprised to find she is pregnant, will mostly and understandably be angry with her, with the father of the child, with his parents. They will be fearful of exposure because they dread the gossip and thinly veiled glee of acquaintances. And they are fearful of the effect of pregnancy and birth on their daughter, and the decision to be made when the baby is born.

Abortion is an obvious way out for the parents. They do not have to tell everyone and can continue to preserve their family privacy. They believe that after the abortion the waters will close over the episode and their daughter will continue with school and all will be 'back to normal'. They will not have to face being grandparents before their time, or face the difficult choice as to whether their grandchild should be adopted. Abortion is a magic duster, wiping away the errors, the tears, the recriminations, the lost innocence. It is expected to help the girl, who will see the error of her ways and break with the undesirable boy. She will go back to school and concentrate on her work. She will be sensible for her own sake and her family's.

As a LIFE counsellor I know that this rarely happens. Abortion ends over three quarters of pregnancies among those under 16 but it does not wipe the board clean. I have repeatedly counselled young girls who became pregnant again within a year or so of abortion, some of whom I counselled in a pregnancy that ended in abortion. Again and again their message is: 'I had one abortion because I was told to, and now I'm older I'm never going through that again'. I have been particularly struck by their resentment that, having had the abortion to put an end to the nagging and pressure, the matter was not closed: 'My mum kept on and on at me about the abortion.' Even the secrecy is not preserved because in most cases the girl's friends will know and talk about the pregnancy and the abortion, and, contrary to what older people may think, there is often a stronger condemnation by her peers of a girl who has an abortion than one who continues pregnancy. The boy may emerge with his reputation enhanced, a kind of 'macho' man, but she is unlikely to escape being called a 'slag'.

There is also the undoubted medical fact that abortion damages future fertility, and the younger the mother is, the more likely such damage will be.

How has the abortion benefitted the young girl? Nothing can undo the fact that she was pregnant or mitigate all that ensues from knowledge of that fact, and her parents' relationship with her is inevitably and permanently altered by the fact of the pregnancy. Their pressure for an abortion may be accepted meekly enough at the time but afterwards become part of a growing feeling on the girl's part of resentment and rejection. If they were instead helped to offer her care and support how much would their mutual love and respect grow. No one would pretend that to be pregnant under 16 causes anything other than problems. But, with the help and counselling that is available, are the problems of carrying on with pregnancy not solvable? And is not abortion, apart from the damage it can do to the young mother's physical health, likely to kill not only the baby but something important for the mother — her right to have the love and support of her parents?

A counsellor knows that there is much practical help available through LIFE and other agencies, voluntary and statutory, for under age mothers and their families. Initially it is important for the wishes and fears of both parents and daughter to be fully discussed. Often in the rush to arrange an abortion there is no true discussion and no one has a chance to say freely what they think or want. The counsellor can offer that chance, as a 'neutral' person, with nothing to gain from the final decision, yet trained to help people to talk about their feelings. It is important that the young girl and her parents, separately and together, tell of their wishes and fears, and sometimes it is only the presence of a LIFE or similar counsellor that allows this. It is possible to offer accommodation during pregnancy if the girl or her parents wish, and this must be arranged in liaison with the statutory services. Education may be continued, indeed should be if the girl is not of school-leaving age. Pro-life groups can help to secure this. The help of professional adoption counsellors should be sought at a suitable stage in pregnancy, not in order to pressurise for adoption, but to allow everyone to examine the facts of adoption and the pros and cons of keeping the baby. It is imperative that anyone who has to cope with this problem should have an up-to-date and comprehensive knowledge of alternatives to abortion (including adoption) within their own area.

Another situation where abortion is usually reckoned to be the lesser of two evils occurs when pregnancy will expose the affair and probably cause an apparently stable marriage and family situation to break up. A variant is where the husband has had a vasectomy so there would be no chance, even if it were advisable, for the wife to pretend that the baby was his. Nowadays most people would recommend that the woman have an abortion, keep her affair secret and decide afterwards whether or not to continue her affair and keep up her apparently stable marriage and family life. Why risk breaking up a family, exposing the lover, wrecking several lives, when abortion solves all?

If she continues the pregnancy it is possible that she will lose not only her lover but her husband and family. She could be left completely alone with her unborn child, to raise that child unaided if she continues pregnancy.

In a complicated situation like this, the woman is under what may be almost intolerable pressures. Perhaps the pregnancy causes her for the first time to face the truth about the damage her affair is doing to herself, her husband and family, as well as her lover. It is only in story-books that long term deception in marriage causes no problems. She may have been deceiving herself anyway about her husband's or, indeed, her born children's ignorance of her affair. She may have deceived herself about her lover's feelings, and be surprised at either his panic-stricken push for her to have an abortion, or his keen wish for her to have 'his' baby.

One thing is sure: abortion will not magically solve the question of whether or not to continue the affair, or help the marriage. The problem of the marriage will still remain. There is a need to look at the totality of the problem in a more comprehensive way, in fact, to have a better chance of solving the couple's underlying problem. If she has an abortion to get out of a tangle, she may well find herself in a deeper mess. She may well lose her lover either through panic because pregnancy occurs, or through disgust provoked by the abortion. She may be so adversely affected emotionally by having an abortion in such a situation that she would not be able to take up family life as though nothing had happened. If she does keep her post-abortion grief to herself to preserve secrecy, it is likely that her unresolved questionings and inability to talk it all out with her husband would lead to further distance and damage to their relationship. Sometimes such pressures are too great to bear and the woman breaks down, and the marriage collapses anyway.

In this situation, when pregnancy was confirmed, a pro-life counsellor would help the woman as well as those near to her to review the alternatives before her, not in order to 'scare' her away from abortion, but to enable her to consider carefully the outcome of whatever decision she eventually makes. She would be given a rare chance to talk in confidence with someone with no emotional or financial interest in the outcome of her decision, who is not there to moralise or condemn her for getting into such a situation, but who is genuinely concerned, woman to woman, to help her to mitigate the damage to herself as well as to her family and lover: one of the outcomes of good counselling is also that she will be helped to acquire skills to cope with difficult situations in the future.

But it is impossible to predict what response the woman's husband or lover will make. The decision to have an abortion is usually made because of the fear that everyone's reaction will be uniformly hostile, threatening, negative, and I stress again that abortion is the counsel of despair, denying those involved the chance to be loving, generous, positive. Abortion relies on a pre-judgement of people and their reaction and motives, pitched at the lowest level of expectation. There is no allowance made for human warmth, love, and the ability to forgive, the chance to grow in deeper understanding after the inevitable hurt and outrage has been expressed.

Those who would counsel abortion to a woman in this kind of predicament should ask themselves who benefits. The unborn child is a clear loser. But so is everyone else, and particularly the woman herself. As with the under 16 pregnant girl, abortion kills something for everyone involved.

Few people, apart from pro-lifers, would question the need to have an abortion if the unborn child is expected or diagnosed as having a handicap. Despite our society's concern and compassion for born people with mental or physical disabilities, there is a double standard which asserts that any disabling condition that can be spotted before birth is reason enough for the child to be aborted. Sometimes even the charities that were founded to support and campaign for children and adults with specific disabilities will also campaign for ever more sophisicated methods of detecting such disabling conditions in the womb — not to cure, but to kill the affected child.

This general climate of opinion of course affects a mother who is told that her unborn child is or may be born handicapped. For some others, particularly older women, it is hard to enjoy pregnancy because of the hurdle of pre-birth screening and tests for handicap. Until at least half way through pregnancy they cannot relax and bond with their unborn baby for fear that these tests might prove positive and the doctors urge abortion.

The introduction of such pre-birth screening is an obvious by-product of the way in which abortion has accustomed us to solve problems. Children with Down's Syndrome are, generally speaking, loving, happy and rewarding to care for. There is growing evidence that certain kinds of therapy, diet, education, can unleash potential that years ago would not have been attained. Yet routine screening in pregnancy, particularly of older women, is aimed at Down's children especially.

A woman who has an abortion because her child is suspected of being a Down's child will have had to make, in mid-pregnancy, a deliberate choice between continuing pregnancy in the expectation of giving birth to a handicapped baby, or the death of a baby that in many cases she will already have felt move in her womb. Such research into the reactions of women after these 'genetic' abortions showed that the grief afterwards is considerable. And that is not to be wondered at. Some women regret the abortion so much that they express a wish to have been 'allowed' to have the baby despite the handicap.

What lies beneath the pressure for her to have an abortion? A primitive fear of deformity lurks in most of us. Aborting the handicapped may masquerade as humanitarian but it abuses our compassion towards suffering and fosters our fear of abnormality. So just when we have made much progress in removing the stigma and guilt feelings attached to handicap, we are putting them back. Of course, it is natural to hope your baby is going to be physically and mentally sound and to be disappointed if he or she is not. We are all a bit frightened of abnormality. We think we will not be able to cope. People talk about sparing us the 'burden' of 'useless' lives. They tell us how a family can be stricken by the arrival of a handicapped child. They go on about 'vegetable existence' and 'quality of life'. They say we cannot afford all those crippled children. This is the kind of subtle or not so subtle pressure exerted on some women in pregnancy. In many hospitals there is little counselling during or after pre-birth screening so that the mother and father are unprepared, and even then are given only a few days at most in which to decide on their course of action. There is rarely any calm time in which they can reflect, examine their own resources and attitudes to the possibility of raising a disabled child, or to consult with experts in the various self-help groups and charities for disabilities.

If, instead, the emphasis were on caring for parents and baby, giving them time, love, statutory help, the approval and encouragement of the rest of society, or the guarantee that, if they cannot bring up their child themselves, there will be loving adoptive or residential care, the parents, and the mother in particular, would not have to judge themselves in haste and without full knowledge. Once again abortion prejudges the issue and assumes that there will be a universal failure to respond lovingly and caringly. Once again the abortion pressure removes much freedom of choice.

And Afterwards

Over the past three or four years there has been a growing awareness by all involved in pregnancy and abortion counselling that women who have had abortions may need counselling afterwards — in some cases long afterwards. The abortion-providing agencies themselves recognise this to the extent that they offer post-abortion counselling. My colleagues and I in LIFE have long been aware of the grief and trauma which some women experience after abortion because a number of women who come for help in pregnancy have had a previous bad experience with abortion.

Until recently there has been a conspiracy of silence about the impact of abortion, but the evidence of an increasing number of academic studies, particularly in America, provides cause for concern. It has been found that many women feel not only immediate sorrow, probably assuaged by relief, after abortion, but longer term grief, difficulty in bonding with children of subsequent pregnancies, resentment against those family and friends who are thought to have urged the abortion, loss of self-esteem, anxiety and disruption of marital relationship.

Some case histories of women helped by post-abortion counselling may illustrate the differing reactions after abortion, and point to the deep need for healing felt by women who have experienced abortion:

Jane was a practising Christian. She did not agree with abortion. When she discovered herself pregnant she was already in the throes of a divorce. This had deeply upset her family and she could not tell them or anyone else of her pregnancy. She opted for abortion. Following it, she felt a period of relief; but soon afterwards, awareness of what she had done began to haunt her. Her divorce behind her, and a new life beginning, she became aware that she had made a hasty decision. She felt alienated from her faith, her family and from herself.

Happily she had the strength to approach a minister who referred her for counselling. During the counselling that followed it was more than apparent that this discussion with the minister was the first major step in her acceptance of what she had done and the first unburdening of her guilt. Now, for the first time she was able to grieve for the baby, and to understand that the suppression of this grief and the anger towards herself was causing the guilt.

The counsellor did not try to mitigate that guilt. Remarks such as 'It wasn't your fault, you were driven to it' would have made matters worse. She shared in the grief, she allowed the client to express all her feelings. She was empathetic to the pain and to the guilt, but made the client feel that she (the client) was totally acceptable to her. Gradually the client was able to accept herself. Regret would always remain but recovery was on the way. She described her return to church as 'going home to a loving family after a very long time'.

Belinda had had an abortion before she was married. Her husband lovingly accepted the situation. In the second year of their happy marriage they started a family, a much-wanted baby. Belinda's depression started then. The birth of the baby, whom they both loved dearly, deepened the depression. She was conscious that by her behaviour she was ruining her marriage.

A chance article on post-abortion grieving prompted her to seek help. The sort of advice that she had been getting from the few friends who knew her circumstances was, 'pull yourself together, you have a wonderful husband, child,' and so on. It did not help.

During her counselling, Belinda had to learn to forgive herself, which she found very difficult to do, and to be able to talk openly about the abortion. This was a tremendous relief and gradually her self-esteem returned. She began to look to the future, not back at the past. She would never be able to cuddle her lost baby but now she mourned openly and so 'found' the baby. She learned that the experiences she had been through could be put to positive use. Her present child and future children will have a very understanding mother.

Belinda's relief did not come overnight, there were still bouts of depression, but the good times in between gradually grew longer.

Sadie had been 14 when she had her first abortion, 16 when she had her second. She was beautiful, artistic and intelligent. By the time she was 18 she was inwardly a mess. Once a lively gregarious girl, she now shunned her fellow-students, she found it difficult to smile, impossible to laugh. When she first visited her counsellor, the latter referred her to the group doctor fearing that she needed psychiatric help. Fortunately this was not the case. She did, however, need very long-term counselling. Sadie blamed herself entirely for the abortions. Her parents would have supported her, as they had done with her sister, who had been faced with the same dilemma and had kept her baby.

There can be little doubt that watching her sister's baby grow up caused much of Sadie's depression, although she deeply loved the child. During the counselling she had to learn to love the child for itself and not for the two babies she had had aborted. She had to learn to like herself again. Able to talk freely with her counsellor, she found herself able gradually to talk to others again. Having finished at college she moved from the area but continued to write on occasions to her counsellor. She finally fell in love and was able to tell her boyfriend all. Peace was a long time coming but happily in the end it did.

Linda was very different from the previous three women. She was not very articulate, although very open. Finding herself pregnant and fearing it was not her boyfriend's baby, she had an abortion at 22 weeks of her pregnancy. She described the abortion in detail to her counsellor and was obviously very shocked by it. Following the abortion she felt very bruised, aching in every limb. She also haemorrhaged badly, which caused some concern. Throughout the counselling she maintained that she had done the right thing, but swore she would never have another and would tell all her friends not to have one.

She conceived again at about the same time her first baby would have been born. Was this compensation for the lost child or was that purely in the counsellor's mind? Certainly, repeat pregnancy is a common pattern among aborted women.

Mrs X was 45 years when she discovered she was pregnant. She was divorced with two teenage children. The boyfriend and close friends suggested abortion. At her age it was a sensible thing to do. Twice she booked, twice she failed to turn up. The third time she walked down the long drive to the clinic longing to turn round and run away, but she continued on. The account that followed was blurred, it had happened five years previously. Sitting in the waiting room she looked at the faces of the other women around her. She again longed to escape but although her brain told her to go, her limbs would not move (the counsellor presumed she had had some kind of pre-med injection).

When she was taken to see the doctor, she remembers saying, 'I don't want this abortion'. Did she really say it or did she imagine she said it? Or did the doctor think she said, 'I don't want this baby'? Or didn't he listen?

She was anaesthetised, and when she woke up it was all over. Over the next few years she would drive out into the country and sit in her car and scream.

A final thought about the effect of abortion upon woman is that it is rarely an experience that can be discussed. A 'successful' abortion is regarded as one that is buried in the past and apparently forgotten. But our growing knowledge of the toll that this secrecy can have on women must make us question further the assumption that abortion benefits women and is the lesser of two evils.

In Conclusion

It is hard to argue that women in this country have noticeably benefitted from abortion. The cost of the grief after abortion, the lost chances for mature development of relationships in families, the increasingly materialistic attitude to sexual behaviour and procreation must be added to the number of unborn children killed. There are no visible tremendous boons for women to compensate.

The Christian response, whether by a trained counsellor or an 'ordinary' person consulted as a friend or relation, to a woman with a problem unwanted pregnancy should be equally caring of her and her unborn child. Abortion harms both mother and baby. The harm to the mother may be very long term and in its working out may damage other members of her family. And, in a way, abortion harms us all. Among those 2 500 000 unborn babies killed since April 1968, could well have been inspiring leaders, artists, writers, scientists, visionaries who could have contributed much to our society. Certainly none of them 'deserved' to die. And their mothers, in most cases being pressurised to have an abortion, have been denied the chance to love them and condemned in many cases to mourn their loss.

Is it not time for all Christians to witness to the dignity and uniqueness of all human life before and after birth, and reject abortion as negative, bloody, violent and degrading, unworthy of the support of Christians?

10

A Counsellor Looks at Abortion

Introduction

The Brook Advisory Centre, which is the only one of its kind in Scotland was very pleased to be invited to make a contribution to this written symposium on the problems surrounding unwanted pregnancy and abortion. It should however be emphasised that the function of the centre is primarily educational and preventive; its objectives are 'the prevention and mitigation of the suffering caused by unwanted pregnancy by educating young persons in matters of sex and contraception and developing in them a sense of responsibility in regard to sexual behaviour'. Pregnancy counselling became part of its work only because of the large numbers of women coming to the Centre who were already pregnant, in distress and unable to find any source of help which would give them the time and support necessary to face the enormous decisions involved. Among these women were, and are, women and daughters of the Kirk (just as their partners were and are its elders, men and sons), as well as women of other denominations and women of no particular allegiance.

To offer an adequate service to clients it was important that both medical and non-medical help were available in one place and that considerable knowledge of other services could be placed at their disposal. Brook was in the fortunate position of having the financial support of the Regional Social Work Committee to pay for the employment of qualified social workers and to have the support of Lothian Health Board in providing the clinic element of the service. Brook is however, a charitable voluntary organisation. It operates within the Law and is answerable for its good practice not only to its funding bodies but to the many members of society in general who support it. Our community is a pluralist one and this is reflected in the staffing of the Centre. In the context of this symposium it may be of interest that the staff includes committed Christians, among them elders of the Kirk.

We had hoped to produce a group response in this Paper but were handicapped by the time scale and although we plan future meetings to consider the issues, this writing is the work of only one person. In thinking and preparing for it I have been greatly helped by three colleagues: Cathie Wright, a social worker; Jane Fraser, a social worker training to be a deaconess in the Church of England; and Gillian Morton, a hospital chaplain.

About Counselling

From the outset it is important to be clear what is meant by the word counselling. It has been heavily used in recent years but without great clarity. Some professions already used the word in the context of giving guidance or 'counsel' but this activity does not have a place in the context of human relationships in which it is now widely used, for example in marriage or bereavement counselling.

Definitions of counselling have been produced in the past few years by the Scottish and British Associations for Counselling. These organisations are committed to the promotion of standards and ethics in the practice of counselling as well as trying to help the public become more aware of how they can make use of counselling skills for their own benefit.

The objectives of counselling and the use of counselling skills are to enable people asking for help, often called clients, to come to decisions about their lives at times of difficulty or crisis, to understand the feelings they experience and why, to acknowledge aspects of their own behaviour which may adversely affect the course of their lives and to recognise that they have the capacity for growth and change within themselves. The teaching of Jesus Christ also assumed that people can change and part of the role of the Church is to offer ways of achieving this.

Some of the qualities identified by Carl Rogers (originator of person-centred counselling) are genuineness, warmth, acceptance, the ability to listen and reflect back accurately, the capacity to be non-judgemental, non-directive and self aware. During meetings between counsellor and client, the counsellor applies the knowledge acquired by theoretical learning as well as by experience, to exploring situations which the client finds difficult. In the course of this, he/she may be able to identify and bring into the open factors which were influencing the client without him/her being aware of this. For instance a young women who knows that her mother loves little children and regrets the family growing up may need to be helped to recognise that her decision to go ahead with an unplanned pregnancy is not because she herself wants a baby but because her mother loves babies and this could be a 'present' for her.

Counselling in an unwanted pregnancy situation calls for the exploration of both immediately accessible information — age, family situation, the nature of the relationship with the father, attitudes to single parenthood, adoption and abortion, religious background and so on — and of less conscious elements like the one already referred to. It may result in a woman, who had

E

been determined to end her pregnancy, continuing with it, or it may lead to a decision to seek abortion. For women who have already made the decision, it gives an opportunity to get a better understanding of their feelings and accept them.

Where I Stand

The Christianity by which I try to live and work is embodied in the teaching and life of Christ which at all times showed care and compassion; he did not necessarily accept the actions of the people to whom he was speaking but Christ unreservedly accepted *them* and extended his love and forgiveness to them, offering his guidelines and hope for the future. We can find this in his own words: 'Judge not that ye be not judged'; 'love your neighbour as yourself' (and in that particularly, we are offered the freedom to take time for ourselves to find out who we are and of what we are made — and to do something about it; for if we hold ourselves in low esteem we will not expect much that is good to happen for us but worse, can we hope adequately to care about our neighbour and see that he/she too gets the best?); 'As ye wish that men would do to you, do so to them' and, another example, 'Let him that is without sin among you cast the first stone'. All are concerned with and addressed to living, breathing, thinking people with the capacity to choose to alter their own behaviour and their own lives.

It is with similar people that Counsellors, and others with a counselling element to their work, are concerned. The men and women — and it must be said that it is mainly women who seek help — with whom I have worked as a Counsellor, have in common the capacity to make choices both moral and practical, to have regard for both themselves and others, and can appreciate the consequences of various courses of action when these are laid clearly before them. My job has been to work with them, to help them see and understand those aspects of themselves which lie beneath the surface, the unconscious. I believe that, just as spirituality is an integral part of our practical everyday functioning, it is also part of our unconscious, woven into millions of experiences, ideas and fantasies. All of these play a part in influencing our decision-making at any time but even more when the decision is of great significance.

As I understand it, the Church's interpretation of the teaching of Christ has not been a static thing. In the Church of Scotland alone there have been schisms and disruptions, usually as one school of thought within the Church tried to temper the assertions of another. If the Church is to have any relevance to the world in which it is working, it must be open to change, but in this generation there are signs that the Church is losing ground. This may have come about because people see inconsistencies in those who condemn policies which allow the taking of the life of an embryo — a potential human being — but stand silent in the face of policies which encourage the accumulation of the means of destruction of whole nations; who insist that severely damaged, helpless creatures are kept alive by enormous input of human and technological effort ... in a society where thousands, able in mind and body, have to struggle to survive. As a Christian I believe that the Spirit of God enables all learning, progress, discovery, that it is only through this intervention that anything can be achieved. I believe too that the teaching of Jesus Christ gave a 'code of good practice' or yardstick against which to measure the way we live. Just as it has taken time to develop science and technology it takes time to acquire the wisdom to make moral decisions on how to use the technology. It may be that we have not grown in wisdom at a sufficient enough rate to keep up with the increasingly difficult decisions required of us but if this is so we gain little by scuttling back to judgements made in an earlier time and different setting. Just as Christ spoke and worked in ways which made sense to the people of his time and environment, we need to have the courage to try to do the same, knowing that he has given us the basic principles.

Absolute statements on the sanctity of life are not helpful to the woman with an unwanted pregnancy, even less if the pregnancy resulted from a sexual assault. She will herself have feelings about ending a pregnancy, derived from her religious background, local attitudes and customs and perhaps from having thought about or discussed these. Many people would say that rather than end a potential human life, women should continue the pregnancies and give the resulting children for adoption. Some of us will have been in this position and know the grief of such a 'bereavement'; unlike bereavement through death, this mourning does not come to any resolution because somewhere, well and happy, or damaged and distressed, our child lives on. Others of us will be the children whose parents were unable to keep us, who were 'given away'. For most of us it is not enough that we simply exist, in a vacuum as it were. We want to know where we come from, not solely in biological terms but in social terms; what our parents and grandparents did, how they looked, where they lived, the colour of their hair, the nature of their personalities. It matters to us that we were wanted and loved and not carried in the womb in a spirit of anguish or resentment. The love and care of parents at its best cannot be bettered as a translation into human terms of the love of God. There cannot be many people today who are unaware of the effects of lack of this love, or worse, of the active rejection of a child.

To give a baby away is such a painful experience, as well as being contrary to the cultural values of many groups in our society, that many young women who continue unplanned pregnancies keep their children. Young single mothers face difficulties over and above those experienced by other groups of single parents and their struggles are regularly attested to by organisations like the Scottish Council for Single Parents and the Royal Scottish Society for the Prevention of Cruelty to Children.

It seems that we are looking at a situation in which there is no perfect solution; a balancing act is involved in which one is striving to find an answer from which least harm will result. Those of us who seek to affirm the ideals of Christianity through physical relationships and recognition of the sanctity of human life (among other things) may have our vision of the Kingdom of God achieved through a humanity which is perfectly fulfilled ... but we also live in the real, imperfect world. As Christ worked from where the people were we can do no better than follow his example. Believing that there is no situation that is so bad that it cannot be redeemed, we take part in counselling which can lead to healing, reconciliation and personal growth which are surely fundamental to the work of the Church.

Abortion

Abortion is not a new phenomenon; it has been referred to throughout history. Prior to the 1967 Abortion Act which enabled women who met certain conditions to have pregnancies terminated, an estimated 100 000 illegal abortions were carried out each year at enormous danger to the lives of the women, many of whom died leaving countless children to grow up as best they could. Despite the risks, women resorted to the back street abortionist, often no more than one of themselves who saw herself as helping out a friend in trouble. In this generation we have removed the risks from abortion, but we have failed to create a society in which women no longer have to resort to it. The necessity for the operation in earlier times, as it often is now, was a desperate bid to enable family life to continue as before without the pressure of an extra mouth to feed or the trauma of family disruption from which there may be no recovery.

When women like Margaret Sanger and Marie Stopes attempted to provide the methods of birth control which could have reduced the number of abortions, they were reviled by their middle-class peers, the majority of whom were at the same time declaring themselves to be upholders of Christian values. In contemporary accounts there is little mention of the Churches taking any positive stance, least of all toward the male partner. The lesson of Onan was learned as masturbation rather than as a possible means of family limitation. Marriage might be a sacrament but what sort of sacrament is it that demands yearly child-bearing regardless of the cost? In our own time the voice of the Church has not been heard clearly in the land proclaiming the value of the lives of women and the importance of contraception to enable them to lead those lives so as to realise their full potential.

Throughout the reproductive life of a sexually active woman (which nowadays may extend from the age of 13–55), a huge number of fertilised eggs are discarded; if this is human life, 'nature' is being unusually profligate. Fetuses which, for one reason or another are recognised by some instinct of the body as unacceptable, spontaneously abort. Thus nature attempts, by its own means, to both protect the mother and guard against disadvantaged babies coming into the world.

Some of the dilemmas faced by those concerned about abortion, centre on the time at which the growing being is invested with 'personhood', or 'ensoulment' as it has also been called. The question has been addressed by eminent theologians who have come to differing conclusions. It is one with which I have considerable difficulty not least because of the need to define what constitutes personhood or soul; is it merely the possession of a human form without capacity for making moral choices? This would embrace the tragic demented creatures who, if unrestrained, would eat their own flesh, disembowel themselves and would never survive in a state of 'nature'; they appear unable to learn and do not recognise that there are moral decisions to be made. We 'do unto them' because they are here in our midst and we see them 'as ourselves'. We have no way of knowing the nature or quality of life they experience. By contrast we are told in a multiplicity of ways what happens in the lives of fully able people who, through accident of birth, are in situations lacking the basics to sustain life. A happily pregnant woman will invest her unborn child with an identity (sometimes having a 'nickname' for it) from an early stage in the pregnancy; an unhappily pregnant woman has no such positive warmth although, for some, fetal movement may set up the beginnings of very ambivalent feelings which can escalate to severe distress. Until recently even a 'wanted' pregnancy which spontaneously aborts was not given recognition through baptism, burial and mourning. There was no acknowledgement of the pain and grief of the parents, particularly the mother; no 'personhood' had been conferred by society whatever the parents might feel.

To me, all this suggests that the value of unborn life and its 'human' qualities are to a considerable extent projected upon it by the mother. If the society in which she lives accepts this and accepts too that there will be instances when the negative feelings of the mother deprive the embryo of its 'being', the problems associated with choosing abortion are reduced. If on the other hand the society confers personhood on the embryo, regardless of the feelings of the person within whose body it must remain for a more or less lengthy period, in order to survive, we have a situation in which the interests of society (rather than of the unborn child) are set against those of the woman. The logical extension to this would surely be that if society insists on survival in this way, the technologies, which are rapidly expanding that which is possible, should be utilised to remove unwanted fetuses from the reluctant womb at the earliest possible moment — currently around 24 weeks — and rear them for whatever glowing future it believes exists. Fetal movement however generally begins around the sixteenth week of pregnancy so that the woman would have an interim period of some two months into which her own feelings would inevitably intrude. We do not have a large sample from which to work but it appears that at least some of the moral outrage expressed at the idea of surrogate motherhood was occasioned by recognition of the affront to the feelings of the surrogate mother. If I am wrong in thinking this I would have to question what in fact the outrage was about; if it was about ownership of the genetic inheritance, a further complication has entered the abortion discussion, whether the male originator of one half of the genetic composition of the embryo has any claim on the whole — the present situation is that he has not — it rests on the assumption that for gestation to be satisfactorily completed most of it must take place in the woman's body, that her life is significantly affected and that she, therefore, has ultimate control over the events which follow confirmation of a pregnancy. By contrast, in the People's Republic of China where the dangers of over-population are clearly recognised, severe sanctions are imposed on women who continue pregnancies which do not accord with the scheme of things agreed by that society. Although a woman there could not be compelled to have an abortion, there would be enormous pressures upon her to set aside her own feelings.

I have already referred to the ambivalent feelings towards the later pregnancy in the woman for whom it is an unwanted event but ambivalence is a significant factor in pregnancy for women: for example, the wife in the infertile marriage who becomes pregnant by another man, who loves her husband and agonises over his possible hurt, may see having a child as a vital part of her own fulfilment and abortion as the unacceptable taking of life; or what about the mother who believes her family is complete and is moving on to another phase in her life but contraception fails and she finds herself pregnant? Contrary to what she would have expected of herself, she is angry and rejecting and above all shocked by her reaction. There is also the case of the childless woman nearing the end of her reproductive life who has a partner with a drink problem by whom she becomes pregnant, who must balance her own desire for a child against her fear that the violence she herself has experienced will be extended to the child; and what about the teenager involved in a loving relationship which leads to pregnancy, which creates such stress that the relationship breaks down, who may not agree with the taking of life but equally believes it is irresponsible to have a child without a father, income or housing?

To end our consideration of this difficult area I shall give examples of the sort of problems being faced. These are not real-life people, but the situations described are real and recurring. As you read I hope you will first be able to put yourself in the place of the 'client' and only then begin to consider what might be the 'best' decision.

Sally is 14, she is 'in care' and lives with community carers who find it very difficult to get some order and routine into her life which has hitherto been chaotic. She does not have any contact with her father who left before she was born. Her mother is trying to cope with two younger children and a job in a pub, which is all she could find which coincided with the hours when she could leave the children with her co-habitee. Sally has become pregnant on her first experience of sexual intercourse with her first-ever boy-friend who is 15.

Netta, aged 37, is married with two teenage children. They are growing up; she is growing older, does not go out to work and has a loving husband. She had been having 'day dreams' about having another baby and may have been a bit less careful than usual about contraception. Discovering that she actually is pregnant and thinking about the implications, she is horror-stricken and finds that she cannot bear the thought of going ahead with the pregnancy. She is even more horrified and shocked by her own feelings and her resentment at the prospect of once again being restricted by the needs of a young child.

Gayle is in her twenties recovering from the upheaval of a divorce two years ago. She has been slowly regaining confidence and has a man friend for whom she has considerable affection; her pregnancy is the result of unexpected intercourse following a pleasant evening out together. As a teenager she had had an abortion following rape by a male member of her family and she has many difficult feelings about this whole area. Her man friend says any decisions are up to her and that although he is not in a position to support her, he will 'stand by' her.

Donna is 16 and on a youth training scheme. She has had her present boyfriend — the first with whom she has made love — for six months and she has talked to him about the possibility of their becoming engaged. Although a few years older, he too is on the YTS project. They use sheaths as contraception and the pregnancy was the result of one of these splitting.

Aged 18, Graham is a first year student at University. He met a female student of his own age at a party, they liked each other and drifted from cuddles to intercourse, but he has not seen her since. A friend has told him she is pregnant but she does not want to see him. He is very unhappy at the thought of 'his' pregnancy being terminated and would really like her to carry on with it. They hardly know each other however and she too is just starting a four year course — the first member of her family to go to University.

Mary is married and the couple are greatly involved in church activites, particularly her husband, who is always available to others in need of help. He is not however a very warm or enthusiastic lover and she often wonders if he notices her at all, except as the mother of their four school-age children.

His cousin from overseas had been staying with them for a couple of months; he clearly admired her, helping with the family, giving her value as a person. Their making love seemed a natural culmination to the relationship which she knew would end when he returned abroad. Neither had dreamed that she would become pregnant.

Although these are all imaginary people, the situation and dilemmas are real enough and have had to be faced by men and women of whom, if we were honest, we might all say 'There but for ... go I'.

Response to Nuala Scarisbrick

It has been difficult to find time to do justice to Mrs Scarisbrick's Paper as Cathie Wright, the social worker who has joined me in writing a response, and I, are both fully involved with working for the Brook Advisory Centre. This is a voluntary organisation committed to trying to help young people avoid making disastrous decisions about their personal lives.

At several points in the paper I found myself wondering if 'counselling', as practised in the pro-life organisations, can be the same activity as counselling as I know it. For instance, when discussing the work of a counsellor in the LIFE organisation, Mrs Scarisbrick refers to the counsellor acting as 'advocate' for the unborn child because those 'advising the mother' are not so concerned. In my understanding, advising and counselling are very different things. Again, later in the text she says, 'most people would recommend that the woman have an abortion'. Some people might indeed 'recommend' this, but they would not be counsellors. Further on still she writes, 'those who counsel abortion to a woman in this kind of predicament', and there she uses 'counsel' as one might use it in the legalistic sense, *ie* of giving counsel, or advice, and again this is to me totally contrary to what counselling seeks to do.

This fundamental difference in interpretation of the word 'counselling' does not however appear to help Mrs Scarisbrick see that if counselling as practised by others exerts pressure, by the same token counselling by pro-life counsellors also exerts pressure.

The neutrality of the counsellor is also referred to: I believe all counsellors would endorse the importance of having a 'neutral' stance with regard to the decisions their clients are trying to reach. This does not mean counsellors do not have views, only that they acknowledge these and as Mrs Scarisbrick rightly says, do not allow them to impinge on the decision-making of the client. It would seem that in not allowing that a decision to ask for an abortion is an acceptable option, pro-life counsellors are in fact making their own interpretation of the word counselling. This makes it as hard for me to accept their stated 'neutrality', as it appears they find it to accept the neutrality of professional people working in settings which do see abortion as a possible choice.

Response to Jean Malcolm

These are several points in this interesting and thoughtful article that I would like to take up.

The first is the description of the unborn child as a 'potential human being', with the strong hint that consequently the child is of less value or importance than the mother or other adults involved.

It is important once again to state that human life begins at conception, *ie* fertilisation.

That is not an opinion, a subject for debate or a matter of religious faith. It is a scientific fact.

Modern genetics and embryology shows that:

(1) Conception begins that process of division, multiplication and then replacement of cells which makes every human body what it is. Before conception there are sperm and ovum. Left to themselves they soon die. Joined together they release an 'explosion' of life, energy, and continuous, purposive development.

(2) At conception the unique genetic 'blueprint' of the new human life comes into being. Every individual receives a genetic inheritance from his (or her) parents, but his own 'blueprint' or 'programme' is different from anyone else's. You and I were genetically complete at conception. That means that at conception the broad outlines of our physiognomy, personality and aptitudes, as well as details like colour of eyes and hair and shape of fingernails, were determined. Since conception we have been steadily becoming the unique new human delineated in our genetic 'blueprint'.

The more we know about conception, genes, deoxyribonucleic acid (DNA) and the complexity of the genetic 'coding' which directs development from the time that the father's sperm meets the mother's ovum, the more obvious it is that conception is the only event I can point to and say, 'That is when I began. That is when I started being me'.

There is no other occasion of which this is true. 'Quickening', as we used to call it, and viability (*ie*, the ability to survive outside the womb), even birth itself, are simply incidents in an already well-advanced process.

They are important incidents, of course. So are learning to walk or talk or getting married — and so on. None of them marks the beginning of life. A child becomes viable, is born, learns to talk, *etc*, because he or she is already alive and growing.

Human life, then, begins at conception and nowhere else (and this is true also of identical twins, even though their individualistion occurs after fertilisation). Human life is a continuous 'becoming' from conception

onwards. So abortion kills a human being. It does not matter when it is done
— six days, six weeks, 16 weeks, six months after conception. Human life is
destroyed on every occasion. It does not matter which link of a chain you cut
— the first, tenth, hundredth or whatever. You break the chain wherever you
do it.

Since human life begins at conception, the victim of abortion — whenever
it is done — is not a merely potential human being. The unborn child is not a
child with plenty of potential, a potential born child or a potential adult. But
he is already actually a human being, because he is already alive and growing
and already the unique human being determined by the unique genetic
blueprint produced at conception.

From conception onwards life is a continuous 'becoming'. The victim of
abortion is already in that process. To say that unborn children are merely
potential human beings is to say that they do not actually exist at all — which
is absurd. It is precisely because they are already alive, growing and human
that abortions are done. A potential life can be prevented. It cannot be, and
does not have to be 'terminated'.

The unborn are at an earlier stage of growth than adults and have greater
potential for development, physical and mental. But everyone has some
potential. No one is a fully realised, a fully achieved human being. From
conception to death, we are all (in varying degrees) actually human and yet
with potential.

The pro-abortion argument is that 6, 12, 18, or 24 weeks old is less
developed than a born person and therefore less human and less valuable.
Therefore a 'fetus' is much less important than a mother.

The first fallacy is that 'less developed' means 'less human'.

I did not develop from an unborn child or fetus. I once was one. I did not
develop from a human embryo. I once was one. I did not develop from a
fertilised egg. I once was one.

If what I was at any of those times had been killed I would not be alive now.
It would have been me who was killed, not a bit of tissue or jelly.

Human life is human life is human life. A human being can be at different
stages of human life, but he can never be 'more human'.

Second, if small is not, after all, beautiful and bigger is, after all, morally
better, why stop at birth? You must go on to say that a five year old is morally
more valuable than an infant, an adult more valuable than a teenager, and so
on. Eventually you must end up by saying that a highly intelligent, middle
class Oxbridge graduate is worth more, morally speaking, than, say a
semi-skilled unemployed middle-aged man or a Calcutta slum-dweller, or
whatever.

Some people are better at certain things than others and therefore more
valuable when those things have to be done.

But we are talking here about moral value — and hence how the law should treat human beings. A civilised society says that all human beings are equal morally and hence before the law. As soon as you start putting a moral price tag on people you have parted company with justice and civilisation.

The second point is the use of the word 'fetus', which to my mind, is an example of how human beings try to obscure truth with words.

'Fetus' is the technical term for the unborn child from 8 weeks onwards. There is no more reason why a layman should use it or why it should be used in everyday speech than there is for calling a new-born baby a 'neonate'. And if it is used, strictly speaking we should specify it and talk of the *human* fetus (because all mammals produce fetuses).

But the pro-abortionist uses it because 'fetus' sounds less human, less real, than 'unborn child'. The word sedates consciences, makes things sound clinical and tidy. It is counter-emotive.

Just because we can call the child 'fetus' does not mean he or she is not also human. Just because we can call a new-born infant a 'neonate', or a woman pregnant for the first time a 'primagravida', does not mean that they are not also human beings.

Let us be honest. It is 'fetus' when we want to get rid of 'it' and 'baby' or 'unborn child' when we want to keep 'it'. Thus the same doctor kills a 'fetus' when he does an abortion but talks about 'baby' to the happily pregnant woman.

If she had wanted an abortion and then changed her mind he would have conveniently changed his vocabulary in mid-stream. Similarly, the 'fetus' who survives abortion suddenly becomes the 'miracle baby' of the headlines.

The third point concerns the use of abortion as a solution to what all of us know are very difficult human dilemmas. I entirely agree with pro-abortion counsellors that there many situations when pregnancy is unwelcome and the overwhelming wish of the pregnant woman or girl and her family is that the clock could be turned back.

But it cannot. Like it or not, a new life has been made and nothing will ever be the same again. To pretend otherwise is to deceive yourself and the woman or girl who seeks counsel. Abortion certainly 'gets rid of' a child whose birth and continued existence may cause great difficulties. But it cannot undo the fact that pregnancy occurred.

In my article I tried to demonstrate that abortion is in itself a problem-causing 'solution' that can corrode and hurt women's emotional and pyschological strength for years after. Abortion not only kills the baby, it damages the mother and, often, those around her. Can there be any human dilemma for which this doubly damaging solution is the only one? Why be defeatist? Why not concentrate on finding positive and loving solutions that do not involve the child's death and mental and/or physical risks to the mother.

For example, the Brook article, alas, took part in the persistent smear campaign against adoption. Abortionists encourage folk to think that no woman could go through pregnancy and then give up her baby. They talk about the 'trauma' of adoption. They relish statistics about high delinquency rates among adopted children, and so on. They reveal typical defeatism here as almost everywhere else.

To decide to go for adoption because it is in the best interests of mother and child, is an admirable and responsible thing. Adoption is one of the positive, loving responses to a situation. Of course, it is not easy. But the degree of trauma depends on the skill of the professional agency involved and on the attitude of those around the mother. Their support is important. The trauma is to some extent in their minds.

The mother will not forget. Why should she? There is nothing to be ashamed of. There is nothing to be flushed out of her life or buried. She has done the best she could for her baby and for herself and should be proud of the fact that her action was based on a realistic appraisal of her situation and the desire to make the best of both lives.

I can propose pro-life help and counsel to apply to all the case histories mentioned in the Brook article. I understand and sympathise with the personal dilemmas in each case and know that a loving, positive and just solution is available that does not include one unborn death and one or more damaged born people.

Appendix 1

BOARD OF SOCIAL RESPONSIBILITY

Deliverance of the General Assembly of the Church of Scotland on the Report of the Board of Social Responsibility.

At Edinburgh, the twenty-first day of May, One thousand nine hundred and eighty-five years —

The General Assembly:
INTRODUCTION
1 Receive the Report of the Board of Social Responsibility and thank the Convener and the Vice-Conveners, Sub-Committee Conveners and Members of the Board, Executive and Office Staff, Field Work and Residential Staff.
2 Express their appreciation of the quality of care given by the Staff of the Board as they seek to meet, in Christ's name, the varied needs of residents in the Homes of the Board.
3 Recognise the important place of Local Committees and congregations in the caring work of the Church, and urge all members of the Church to be aware of the vital part they may play in care and in the healing of divisions.
4 Instruct the Board of Social Responsibility to consult with Presbyteries and other agencies to consider and where possible introduce ways in which the Church may cater for the social and spiritual needs of the unemployed in our communities and to report the results to the next General Assembly.

IN NEW DEVELOPMENTS
5 Hear with pleasure of the Board's success at Williamwood House, and of its proposed development of work for the confused elderly in Inverness and Polmont.
6 Learn with interest of the spread of caring for mentally ill people and record their gratitude to the Alexander Forrester-Paton Memorial Housing Association Ltd for the gift of Gaberston House, Alloa.
7 Instruct the Board to invite and encourage Kirk Sessions to consider ways of involving congregations and members in the continuing care of the mentally handicapped and their families within their parishes.
8 Commend the Board's initiative in tackling the growing problem of drug addiction, and thank Britoil for its generous donation to this work, to establish the Rainbow Centre in Glasgow.
9 Note the continuing difficulties occasioned by the changes in sources and methods of funding, and commend the efforts of Executive Staff in seeking to ensure continuity of appropriate care for all residents.
10 Regret that the initiative taken by the Secretary of State for Wales in the

provision of adequate funding for the mentally handicapped is not reflected in the funding provided in Scotland, and that the provision for the mentally ill in Scotland is much less than in England and urge the Secretary of State for Scotland to make such provision for the mentally handicapped that is proportionate to provision made to other parts of the United Kingdom.

11 Welcome the growth of international relationships with Christian social work agencies in Germany, the Netherlands, Sweden and the United States of America, and exchanges of staff with counterparts in Germany and Sweden.

IN SOCIAL WORK

12 Recognise the Board's flexible response to rapidly changing needs, its adaptation of buildings for change of use, and welcome the improvement in the granting of Planning Permission.

13 Commend the contribution of the Church to education in List D Schools, and note the uncertainty which exists with regard to management and funding.

14 Express their appreciation of the rehabilitation work done for those addicted to alcohol and other drugs, and of the family counselling units now operating in Simpson House, and the Tom Allan Centre.

15 Learn with gratitude of the work in forty-one Homes for the care of the elderly, noting the need to increase staff to cope with the growing frailty of residents who are living longer and encourage the Board to continue calling upon HMG to review immediately the arbitrary reductions made in board and lodging charges allowable by DHSS for elderly persons being admitted to Residential Homes and Nursing Homes.

16 Welcome the steady emphasis on staff training, the large number of placements of University and College students in our Homes, and the Board's involvement in the Youth Training Scheme.

17 Record their appreciation of those who have supported the work of the Board by legacies and donations, thus enabling development to take place.

IN SOCIAL INTERESTS

18 Recognise that while alcohol continues to be the single most abused drug in Scotland, note with concern the increase in the use of illicit drugs and urge HM Government to provide resources for employment, education and leisure activity so that young people may enjoy purposeful living.

19 Receive the report on abortion and, reaffirming that on Biblical and historic Christian conviction the fetus is from the beginning an independent human being, conclude that its inviolability can be threatened only in the case of risk to maternal life, and that after the exhaustion of all alternatives.

20 Are aware of the ethical issues, the hard moral choices, and the pain felt by all involved in cases of pregnancy termination, especially the pregnant women themselves, and ask the Church to support with compassion those in this situation.

21 Urge local congregations to provide within a caring community a healthy and welcoming environment and counselling facilities for young people.

22 Commit the Church to securing a review of the 1967 Abortion Act.

23 Receive with interest the comments of the Board on the Report of the Committee of Inquiry into Human Fertilisation and Embryology (the Warnock Report) regretting the failure of the Report to give adequate consideration to the moral questions raised by the various medical solutions offered to couples facing the problems of infertility and childlessness.

24 Note the Board's acceptance of AIH (artificial insemination by husband) and *in vitro* fertilisation (IVF), and support the Board's rejection of AID (artificial insemination by anonymous donor), egg donation, embryo donation, and surrogacy, which are incompatible with the Christian concept of marriage.

25 Welcome the Warnock Report recommendation that counselling should be available to all infertile couples and third parties at any stage of treatment for infertility.

26 Reject all non-therapeutic embryo experimentation as being contrary to the Christian belief in the sanctity of human life.

27 Commend to the Church the continuing study of the moral issues raised by the directions currently being taken by medical science in the area of human reproduction.

28 Instruct the Board of Social Responsibility to prepare a report on Natural Family Planning and present it to a future General Assembly.

29 Receive with interest the report of the Committee on Health and Healing and commend to the Church the recommended literature and publications.

30 Recognise that the Healing Ministry is part of the total ministry of the Church, and urge Presbyteries and congregations to acknowledge this fact, and to provide support and understanding for its fulfilment.

31 Receive with concern the report on the needs of those engaged in the Parish ministry and urge Presbyteries to participate in the planned Consultation on these matters.

32 Commend to ministers and congregations that section of the Report which emphasises the needs of people involved in the caring services and ask them to consider ways of offering support and understanding to workers in these services with whom they are in contact.

33 Hear with concern of the prevalence of community breakdown and disease and its causes, and commend to all urban congregations for consideration the suggestions for action made in the Report.

34 Urge HM Government to consider the needs of areas of multiple deprivation with a view to recommending selective reversal of financial cuts because of their vulnerability to reductions in social and community services.

35 Welcome the guidelines provided for those involved in the Healing Ministry and commend them as an acceptable code of conduct.

36 Thank and discharge the Committee on Health and Healing as set up in 1980, and proceed to set up a Committee within the Board of Social Responsibility as suggested in the Report.

IN GENERAL

37 Express appreciation of the continuing work of the Women's Council of the Board of Social Responsibility, particularly in giving publicity to and focusing support for the work of the Board through Woman's Guild branches and Young Women's Groups.

38 Note the success of the Board's publicity through audio-visual aids, Press coverage, and the wide distribution of the 'Circle of Care' calendar, and appoint 21 September 1986 as Social Responsibility Sunday.

39 Note that the Board has followed the instruction of the General Assembly of 1984 relative to the Petition of Busby East Parish Church and awaits the final outcome of the case.

40 Record appreciation of the service of the Revd T Morton, Convener, and Mrs

Nita Alexander, Vice-Convener, whose term of office comes to an end at this time.

41 Receive with interest the supplementary statement of the Kirk Care Housing Association Ltd.

3.2 Study Group on Abortion

1 *The Christian Starting-point.* From the beginning, the Church of Scotland's concern has been to start with the question of principle. Under the head 'The Supreme Question', the report to the 1966 General Assembly stated 'we cannot assert too strongly that the inviolability of the fetus is one of the fundamentals and its right to life must be strongly defended'. We re-affirm this assertion on several grounds: the biblical teaching, in which the unborn child is regarded as bearing the divine image; the assertion of the creed that Jesus Christ was 'conceived by the Holy Ghost', God taking manhood to himself *in utero*; the unbroken tradition of the Christian Church, whereby the first Christians took over the strong Jewish antipathy to abortion; and the discoveries of modern genetics and embryology, which confirm us in our belief that the fetus is an independent being, a tiny member of our species.

We believe that in consistent application of the principle laid down in the 1966 report there lies the key to our response to abortion today.

2 *The Practice of Abortion.* We are therefore appalled by the fact that since the passage of the 1967 Abortion Act more than two million unborn children have been aborted. In particular, the annual number of abortions being carried out in Scotland has continued to show a slow but inexorable rise, increasing from 7283 per annum in 1977 to 8419 in 1983; this means that 162 abortions a week are carried out in Scotland (Annual Report of Registrar General, Scotland, 1983). Disregard of the Christian principles of family life, a shallow view of sexuality, and pressures from groups in society which are committed to values very different from our own, have led enormous numbers of women and girls to seek an end to their pregnancies. The effect of this has, apart from anything else, been a cheapening of our society's general regard for human life. In effect, the Act has brought about 'abortion on demand', in that terminations are rarely refused those who diligently seek them. This is an intolerable abdication of society's obligation to protect the weakest and most helpless members of the species.

Under the terms of the 1967 Abortion Act, there are four grounds under which termination of pregnancy may be carried out.

(a) When 'the continuation of the pregnancy would involve risk of injury to the physical or mental health of the pregnant woman, greater than if the pregnancy were terminated'.

The vast majority of terminations are justified on this ground.

In 1981, 96.3 per cent of all abortions in Scotland were carried out under this clause of the 1967 Act. While there are a few cases where there is clear evidence of severe physical or mental illness, the interpretation of what consists a 'risk to the physical or mental health of the pregnant woman' is so wide that this clause has been used to justify 'abortion on demand'. Under this clause abortions are carried out in response to a wide variety of problems. In a large number of cases, pregnancy has occurred in a young unmarried girl who has been abandoned by her boyfriend at the news of the conception. The girl often feels unable to confide in her parents and seeks pregnancy termination as a solution to her problem. In other cases, pregnancy may occur as a result of contraceptive failure and threaten the career and the life-style of the woman. The problem may be compounded when the family's standard of living is dependent upon the wife's income. Again, pregnancy may occur, by mistake, in an older woman who has completed her family many years ago and she may feel unable to cope with the prospect of a second young family. Many other such circumstances are used to justify abortion on the grounds that they threaten the mental health of the mother.

While these problems are real to the individuals concerned, there is no doubt that, under this clause, many abortions have been carried out to prevent social inconvenience or to protect against the consequences of irresponsible or casual sexual behaviour. It is the abuse of this clause in the 1967 Abortion Act that has led to widespread public concern, among Christians and many non-Christians alike. There can be no doubt that the majority of abortions which are done under this clause were not envisaged as justifiable by the legislators who passed the 1967 Abortion Act. This misuse of the Abortion Act requires the urgent attention of legislators to ensure that the original intentions of Parliament are reflected in actual practice.

It is also important to recognise that abortion to relieve social distress may create more problems than it solves because many women develop feelings of guilt and unhappiness after an abortion. After an initial period of distress at the realisation of an unexpected pregnancy, many women come to accept the situation and an initially unwanted pregnancy may later be a much loved child. This means that, for many women, continuation of the pregnancy proves to be a much better long term solution than the apparently 'easy option' of pregnancy termination.

Two specific arguments, which are used to defend this clause in the 1967 Act, need specific mention. The first is that a reduction in the number of legal abortions would lead to a rise in illegal abortions, with unhappy consequences for the mothers concerned. While no one wishes to see a return to the practice of back-street abortion, the prevention of one evil cannot be used as a justification for another. What is needed is, first, a much more responsible attitude to sexual behaviour, so that unwanted pregnancy does not occur in the first place and, second, a more caring response by society to enable women to continue with their pregnancies.

The second argument is that abortion is justified in cases when pregnancy has occurred following rape. Undoubtedly, this is a situation which arouses great compassion for the plight of the women concerned. In practice, difficulties can sometimes arise from the fact that the medical decision to terminate has to be made against the background of uncertainty about whether the pregnancy is indeed the result of rape. When rape has occurred, the psychological damage to the innocent mother is very great, and many Christians would regard this as justification for abortion. The unborn child, however, is also an innocent party, and its destruction cannot undo the evil which has already been done.

The main argument that is advanced in defence of abortion is that termination of pregnancy may relieve suffering in the pregnant woman or in some cases, in her family as well. From our belief in the sanctity of all human life we are convinced that the inviolability of the fetus can be brought into question only in the case of risk to maternal life and when all alternatives have been exhausted. We recognise that some Christians, whether as patients or as members of the medical or nursing profession, may face certain dilemmas when they encounter the practical problems of an unwanted pregnancy. It is therefore necessary to discuss further the practical grounds on which abortion is advocated and the general argument that the relief of suffering is a justifiable defence of abortion in some circumstances.

(b) When 'the continuation of pregnancy would involve risk to life of the pregnant woman, greater than if the pregnancy were terminated'.

We recognise that, on rare occasions, the life of the mother can be seriously threatened by the continuation of the pregnancy. In such circumstances, it may be necessary, if the mother so wishes, for the pregnancy to be terminated, although, when possible this should be delayed until the child has a chance of survival. This ground for termination is used in 0.3 per cent of all cases of abortion. While we recognise that this involves a small proportion of all terminations, we would urge for the strictest vigilance so that interpretation of this ground may not itself be trivialised.

(c) 'The continuance of the pregnancy would involve risk of injury to the physical or mental health of the existing children of the family of the pregnant woman greater than if the pregnancy were terminated.'

This clause of the 1967 Act is used as the main justification for abortion in 1.8 per cent of cases. The purpose of this clause was to ameliorate the consequences of acute difficulties due to social deprivation. All Christians must be concerned with the problem of social deprivation but the solutions should be sought in terms of practical help. Abortion of the child does not necessarily solve the problems of deprivation and, indeed, by creating feelings of guilt, may further damage a family unit which is already under stress. The Christian response should be that greater help must be given to those agencies who strive to relieve suffering associated with social deprivation.

(d) 'There is a substantial risk that if the child were born, it would suffer from such physical or mental abnormalities as to be seriously handicapped.'

This clause is used to justify abortion in 1.6 per cent of cases. There can be no doubt that this clause poses very sharp ethical dilemmas for many parents. In some cases, a proven abnormality may be shown by clinical investigation, and the parents may seek abortion, hoping to have a normal child in a subsequent pregnancy. In other cases, there may only be a probability of fetal abnormality. This may occur after German Measles injection in pregnancy where there is a possibility, but not a certainty, of some degree of physical or mental abnormality. Again, there may be an inherited risk of an abnormality; for example, muscular dystrophy affects only boys so that male children are aborted to ensure that only normal female offspring are produced. Considering the distress caused by an abnormal pregnancy, great understanding must be extended to the parents involved.

The issues are, however, complex. When there is only a probability of an abnormality, this means that many normal pregnancies will also be aborted. There is also a wide spectrum of what constitutes an abnormality. At the most severe end, there are conditions which are incompatible with life after birth and abortion merely brings forward the inevitable to shorten the parents period of distress while the mother carries the baby. At the other end, there may be abnormalities which are still consistent with a happy and useful life. Even when there is an inevitability of mental handicap, as with a Down's Syndrome child, the life of the child may bring happiness to the family concerned.

While recognising the difficulties associated with an abnormal pregnancy, Christians cannot condone abortion in all circumstances because abortion does not prevent handicap, it merely destroys those who are already its victims.

3 *The Sanctity of Life and the Relief of Suffering.* The problem of abortion is often seen in the wider context of tension between the two basic principles under which medicine has traditionally been practised: the sanctity of human life, and the relief of suffering, both prime Christian concerns. It is said that there are occasions when the latter should take precedence over the former, such that the likely future suffering of the child (as yet unborn), or the mother, or the rest of the family, or indeed the pregnant woman's present distress, or some combination of these factors, may predominate over the sanctity of the child's life and its claims on the physician.

There are a number of problems with such a moral analysis:

(a) Its implications
(i) It requires that in circumstances other than those related to the abortion issue the sanctity of a life which is not otherwise in jeopardy may be subordinated to the relief of suffering.

(ii) It requires, moreover, in many cases, that the relief of the suffering of one person may over-ride the *sanctity of life of another*.

These are momentous implications, particularly since the concept of 'suffering' is so broadly drawn.

(b) Its foundations
(i) 'Sanctity of life' and 'relief of suffering' are not competing moral principles *since they are principles of different kinds*. The sanctity of life arises out of the nature of human existence as bearing the image of God. It is therefore the basic assumption of all our inter-personal relations. The vocation of the physician is to relieve the suffering of people in a way appropriate to the nature of people, as a special case of the obligation laid upon us all to behave toward our fellow men and women in love and compassion.

(ii) The obligations to relieve suffering and to respect the sanctity of life are compatible only on the assumption that *the taking of life is not a possible treatment for the relief of suffering*. Qualifying the sanctity of life in order to relieve suffering has the effect of nullifying the principle and entails the implications spelled out above.

We are therefore required by the fact that men and women are made in the image of God to uphold the sanctity of human life and to resist any suggestion that, in the interests of the relief of suffering, any human life (whether that of the sufferer or of another person who is in some way causing suffering) may be forfeited, by the decision of a physician or at the request of any other individual.

4 *Alternatives to Abortion*. It is not enough for the Church to condemn the widespread practice of abortion. Practical and sympathetic counselling and help are required by those confronted with the awful dilemma, under such pressure to conform to expected social patterns and to dispose of their unborn children. Any woman seeking a termination should be able to consult a responsible medical practitioner or other professional person who is able to provide counselling services. It is essential that the counsellors should have sufficient time to spend with the woman, or preferably the couple; and it may often be the case that a medical practitioner has insufficient time to devote to each individual case. In these circumstances, another person, such as a social worker, may be a more appropriate counsellor. It is essential that positive alternatives to abortion be adequately explored with the pregnant woman. We believe that, at present, the balance is against unmarried mothers especially being able to continue their pregnancies both on social and economic grounds.

There are independent, charitable agencies already working in this field, though they are greatly outstripped in size and resources by other agencies which readily counsel in favour of abortion. We need to develop and encourage counselling services which can also give practical help and offer, for example, accommodation to those whose continued pregnancies require it. The Christian, the congregation and the national Church are all alike called to bear witness against the practice of abortion by their involvement in the provision of alternatives, helping with problem pregnancies and encouraging adoption for those children whose mothers cannot cope with the prospect of further additions to their families, also welcoming single parents and their children into the midst of congregational life.

5 *Conscientious Objection.* At this juncture, many years after the introduction of the 1967 Abortion Act, we deplore the failure in implementation of the intentions of that Act regarding those who have a conscientious objection to participation in termination. It is plain to those involved that the provision of the 1967 Act for medical and nursing staff to opt out of abortion work without prejudice to their careers has not worked well and that greater protection is required for Christians and others who find themselves in this position, and if conscientious men and women are not to be discouraged from entering the gynaecological field (as was feared in the Lane Committee submission of 1975).

Recommendations
1   That the Church be asked to reaffirm the biblical and historic Christian conviction in the sanctity of all human life and that, from the beginning, the fetus is an independent human being, made in the image of God.
2   That the Church be asked to conclude from this conviction that the 'inviolability of the fetus' (1966 report) can be threatened only in the case of risk to maternal life and after the exhaustion of all alternatives.
3   That the Church be aware of the practical difficulties which confront those in the medical profession in the exercise of their work particularly through pressure of time and encourage continued discussion both within and outwith the profession of the ethical issues involved in cases of termination.
4   That the Church be asked to consider ways in which alternatives to abortion can be put to those with difficult pregnancies, and support provided for them, by the encouragement of voluntary agencies and where appropriate by clearly rendering existing counselling facilities available to those in need, also by providing accommodation and other practical assistance where necessary.
5   That local congregations recognise and develop their opportunity for providing a healthy environment in which young people may develop caring and responsible relationships, involving all members of the Christian family, and in which handicapped children or adults would find a role as equal members.
6   That the Church commit itself to securing a review of the 1967 Abortion Act.

3.3 Report of the Committee of Inquiry into Human Fertilisation and Embryology
(WARNOCK REPORT)
The Committee of inquiry into human fertilisation and embryology, chaired by Dame Mary Warnock, DBE, was established in July 1982 with the following terms of reference:

'To consider recent and potential developments in medicine and science relating to human fertilisation and embryology; to consider what policies and safeguards should be applied, including consideration of the social, ethical and legal implications of the developments; and to make recommendations.'

The report of the Committee was published in July 1984 and responses were invited from a wide range of groups, including the Churches.

In making its response, the Board has been glad to apply many of the principles established in the British Council of Churches — Free Church Federal Council Report, 'Choices in Childlessness', which received the commendation of the General Assembly in 1982. 'Choices in Childlessness' sets out most helpfully the context within which, the Board believes, the present discussion of the recommendations of the Warnock Committee should be placed. In accepting its findings the General Assembly has called Church members, in seeking to follow the will of God, to have a sensitive awareness of the experience of childless couples.

Childlessness is a problem which faces one in ten couples, resulting for many in bitter disappointment. As the Childlessness Report points out, some couples experience profound grief as they mourn for the child which they cannot bear. Their personal desire to have a child will also derive, however, from social expectations, for we all affect and are, in turn, affected by the world in which we live. Thus, infertile couples' sense of loss may be only aggravated by the attitudes and expectations of friends and family who, unthinkingly, assume that they should conform to the accepted pattern of child-bearing. In posing the question of the limits and limitations which should be recognised in the development of infertility treatment, the Warnock Report has faced the Church and Church members afresh with the need to respond appropriately to the human as well as the moral implications in this area.

The Board of Social Responsibility made a submission to the Committee during its inquiry. It followed this with a response to the report in which it indicated its very real concern about the recommendations contained therein and the understanding of human life which they represent. The full text of the Board's response, which embodies principles accepted by the General Assembly on previous occasions, is given below:

'The Board of Social Responsibility recognises that under the terms of its remit the Committee of Inquiry into Human Fertilisation and Embryology has been given responsibility for reporting on an issue of profound significance for modern society. The Board welcomes publication of the Committee's report as an important development in discussion of ethical questions presented by advances in science and medicine in the area of human fertilisation and embryology.

Believing firmly in the duty of all responsible groups to contribute to the moral context within which new techniques are developed and implemented, the Board welcomes the opportunity to respond to the Committee's findings. In doing so, however, the Board would stress at the outset its deep concern over the failure on the part of the Committee of Inquiry to consider moral questions relating to the status of human life, from which indeed ethical questions concerning the treatment of human tissue arise. It is invidious to elevate the interests of knowledge and technique over consideration of the subject matter, even in relation to as worthy a cause as the relief of infertility, without at least discussing the grounds on which such a choice may be made. This, the Board believes, the Committee has done. The public disquiet over the pace of developments in these areas which is said to have led to the establishment of the Committee is taken to be confined to the practical implications of scientific advance in relation to human fertilisation and embryology and their social and legal consequences. No consideration is given to the morality of acts in this area *viz,* its decision to isolate its discussion from questions arising in relation to legislation on abortion or contraception and underlying moral issues.

The Board finds that it is impossible to sympathise with the recommendations of the Warnock Committee without conceding issues of principle which the Church considers to be of fundamental importance to its understanding of human life within the created order and to the Gospel of Jesus Christ. The Board would offer as the basis of its comments the following points — from its acceptance of transcendent moral values, man made in the image of God, redeemed through Christ:

1   The Christian perspective starts from the position that human beings have been created by God and are loved by God. Made 'in the image of God and after his likeness', man is unique and has been endowed with faculties which enable him to enter into a personal relationship with his creator, and undertake responsibility for the

creation on behalf of and alongside his creator. However, it is not just to the creative activity of God we must look, but to the Incarnation and of his saving activity. God in Christ underlines not only the uniqueness of man, but the attitude of God, which is that His love does not depend on our achievements or abilities. The value of human life and the dignity of life, derive from how God regards and treats us, and not on any status which legal or moral codes and conventions may confer at particular ages and stages of development. Thus, human beings may never treat each other as means to ends, but only as ends, and as ends backed by ultimate sanction of God's own being and love incarnate in Jesus Christ. No human being at any stage in his or her development may be treated in a way that violates his/her distinctively human nature and status, or subjects him/her to being a means to an end, even where that end is the greater health and happiness of other beings.

2   From the moment of conception the human embryo is genetically complete. It is an 'organised, unique, living unity with intrinsic capacity for development, human in character from its beginning' (Dr Teresa Iglesias). The moral status of the embryo and its moral claim on us do not diminish the further back we go in the stages of its development. From the moment of fertilisation it has the right to be protected and treated as a human being. There is 'a serious ambiguity about an argument from the premise that the embryo is 'potentially human', for the potentiality concerned is not that of becoming something else but of becoming what it essentially is' (Prof. T F Torrance).

General Comment
Failure to address itself to the status of the embryo, the question at the heart of its inquiry, leads the Committee to describe a form of scientific endeavour which many scientists would not support. It isolates science from its subject matter. Human life is intrinsically meaningful: it is to be understood in terms of the will and purpose of God involving mutual obligation within society.

Thus the practice of scientific inquiry which assumes neutrality in its treatment of human life is a delusion. Equally, a report from a Committee of Inquiry concerning the practical implications of techniques in human fertilisation and embryology which fails to confront moral issues arising for science and society from this practice is practically irrelevant. The Committee missed the opportunity to inform medical practice and scientific inquiry from insights regarding the nature of their inquiry and its consequences in terms of ethical prescriptions. Much more seriously, the Committee has chosen to advocate for medical and scientific purposes practices which are based on an understanding of the status of the embryo which is unexamined but which denies its essential humanity.

The elevation of the requirements of infertility treatment above concern for the welfare of human embryos is to adopt a utilitarian perspective from which the newly created life, which is the embryo, is to be seen as a means to an end. This is to deny the status of human life as an end in itself, each individual made in the image of God, and independent reality in a special relationship with him through Jesus Christ. The utilitarian criteria employed throughout the Report too often result in the inherent right and claims of the embryo at all stages in its existence, being discounted in favour of ends that are deemed to serve 'the public good'. The Board holds as fundamental the position indicated by the World Medical Association in its 'Declaration of Helsinki' (1964 and 1975): 'In research on man the interests of science and society should never take precedence over considerations related to the well-being of the subject'.

Often the Report comes near to the position expounded by Dr Edwards, that what is acceptable to most must be taken as right '... in a society which sanctions the abortion of a fully-formed fetus, the discarding of such a minute, undifferentiated embryo should be acceptable to most people.' The Committee's recommendations with regard to the creation, use and disposal of embryos is clearly a legacy of abortion legislation which has effectively eroded any real claim to life on the part of the embryo. Indeed it is fair to say that the Committee's recommendations embody a greater sensitivity for the experience of the embryo than has been shown hitherto; but because those recommendations are based on a view of the embryo which does not see it as intrinsically human, they inevitably diverge in ways which can only be supported by a utilitarian view, *eg*, the production of spare embryos for the purpose of research. It is sad that in choosing to not engage in a discussion of moral values the Committee missed the opportunity to consider in the context of modern developments fundamental issues arising in this field as in the related one of abortion.

Related to the Committee's recommendations on the treatment of the embryo is its consideration of the context within which infertility treatment might be carried out. Profound as feelings associated with infertility unquestionably are, the experience of infertility should not be taken to advocate practices such as AID, embryo transfer or egg donation which imply either the introduction of a third party into the marriage relationship or treat women as merely incubators or men as disinterested donors of sperm. In this report the introduction of licensing arrangements and legal adjustments is used to sanction activities and to build practices into our social structure which are possible through science but which show no concern for moral issues relating to marriage or family life. The Board would here reaffirm its belief in marriage as the relationship in which human sexuality may be fulfilled. Methods of overcoming childlessness should therefore be directed only to helping married couples (see detailed comments).

In its concern to build scientific possibilities into our social and legal framework, the Committee has given no thought to the experience of infertility as at least partially a social phenomenon. Nor does it consider alternative means to the relief of infertility, which would not involve the sacrifice of embryos as an experimental resource. It seems a pity that the Report does not consider more fully alternative ways of learning about and treating hereditary disease and congenital abnormalities *etc*, and did not look at research being carried out by people like Professor Jerome Lejeune. Work being done in this area clearly merits closer consideration under the terms of the Committee's remit.

Detailed Comment
While re-emphasising its concern for the protection of human life at all stages of its development and for recognition of exclusivity in the marriage relationship, the Board would offer the following detailed comments on the Report:

1 *Counselling*. The Board welcomes the Committee's emphasis on counselling. It has been noted that recommendation 19, based on paragraphs 3.3 and 3.4 makes provision for counselling to be available for all infertile couples and third parties at any stage of treatment as an integral part of NHS and private sector provision. The Board would propose strengthening this recommendation to refer, as the relevant paragraphs do, to fully trained counsellors.

2 *Marriage*. Where the Committee states that all its recommendations refer to infertility treatment for couples living together in a stable hetero-sexual relationship, the Board would propose that methods of overcoming childlessness should be directed only to married couples.

3 *Artificial Insemination.* The Board would here distinguish between artificial insemination by husband (AIH) and artificial insemination by donor (AID). The Board sees no objection to fertilisation of the ovum of a wife by the sperm of her husband through artificial means when it is difficult or impossible in the normal way. By contrast it sees in AID the unwarranted intrusion of a third party in the marriage relationship, which it cannot support.

4 *Registration of AID Children.* The Board recognises that AID is established as an aid to infertility. It recognises furthermore that developments in this field have presented serious legal anomalies. The Board would emphasise that recommendations offered in the Report as a means to resolving the status in law of AID children leave unresolved the tensions which may face any family through the involvement of an 'absent parent'. It is to be questioned whether counselling and support such as are offered in cases of adoption will meet problems which arise subtly through AID.

The present arrangements for registering a child born as the result of AID involve a legal fiction. The Report recommends that the law should be changed so as to permit the husband to be registered as the father (Recommendation 53). While this recommendation is welcomed so far as it goes, it is not entirely clear from the Report that a change in the law as such will remove the implicit deceit which is currently present in registration. There is some doubt about the desirability of adding the words 'by donation' to the father's parental description. Rather than simply changing the law to accommodate AID the whole basis and procedures for registration of births and parentage should be examined.

5 *AID Donors.* The Board believes that the Committee has not recognised sufficiently the real responsibility of the donor in this transaction. The most stringent of safeguards should be applied for the protection of the child and the couple involved in the donation.

6 *In Vitro Fertilisation.* As a technique to relieve infertility within the husband/wife relationship, IVF raises no moral questions. However, when superovulation is used to produce more embryos than will be transferred to the mother's uterus, questions arise concerning the deliberate creation of new life without hope of its potential being realised. As the report has indicated the opinion of the medical profession on the whole is that in the present state of knowledge, superovulation is very desirable (5.7). The Board would urge that discussion of the ethics of producing spare embryos in IVF should be included in any discussion of the ethics of experimentation on embryos.

Any discussion of IVF and its consequences should consider how developments in this area relate to other means of overcoming childlessness which is the result of tubal blockage. In addition, consideration should be given to the degree of priority which might be accorded to the couple's interests within the context of IVF.

7 *Egg donation and Embryo donation.* It is the Board's view that egg donation and embryo donation raise similar moral problems in relation to marriage as AID. It can therefore not support their development as valid techniques to aid infertility.

8 *Licensing Authority.* The Board would argue that before any such licensing authority was established further consideration should be given both to the status of the human embryo and to the context of infertility in relation to which it would seek to operate. The Board is not satisfied that sufficient discussion has taken place thus far to prepare the way for licensing arrangements.

The recommendations concerning the function of a statutory licensing authority to regulate research and infertility services are generally to be welcomed. The Recommendation concerning lay representation should be strengthened to provide for a lay majority on the licensing authority including representation from the Christian

Church. As it stands the recommendation suggests that lay representation should be 'substantial' but that is not sufficiently clear.

9   *Embryo Experimentation.* From its belief in the inviolability of the human fetus, the Board rejects the production of spare embryos, or research on embryos (within any time period), in addition to those practices ruled out by the Committee (Chapters 10-13). No embryos should be brought into existence purely for research nor should research be carried out on embryos which happen to come into existence in the course of other experiments. The Board would here call for a halt on all experimentation on human embryos, and would accordingly lend its support to Expression of Dissent B.

The Board would here endorse the call with which it has been glad to associate itself, for an immediate moratorium on all experimental works which are not a part of treatment designed to improve the life prognosis of and benefit to each and every individual human embryo so exposed.

10   *Storage of Embryos.* The Board notes the recommendations for the storage of human embryos. It would propose that couples should be consulted from the beginning about the storage and disposal of embryos. Storage of embryos should be undertaken only to facilitate conception. Embryos should be destroyed after couples indicate that they have no wish for additional children. Embryos should be destroyed where the marriage relationship ends for any reason or where there is no agreement between the couple over their use (see Recommendation 33).

11   *Disposal of Embryos.* The use of words 'disposal' and 'dispose' (*eg,* in Recommendation 31, 32 and 33) is ambiguous. They should be replaced by the words 'destruction' and 'destroy', to avoid any possibility that anyone should think that embryos could be disposed of by means of sale.

12   *Surrogacy.* The Board would re-assert the view of the Report of the British Council of Churches — Free Church Federal Council Working Party, on which it was represented and with which it has associated, that surrogacy is 'demeaning to both mother and child' and that it should be made illegal (Choices in Childlessness 1982).

The Board welcomes the recommendations of the Report in regard to surrogacy. However, it would point out that surrogacy in fact differs only in detail, and not at all in principle from other techniques involving a third party in the marriage relationship of husband and wife.

13   *The Church.* The Board would take this opportunity to commit itself afresh to promoting within the Church of Scotland the 'Reminders and Recommendations' which form Chapter 7 of the 'Choices in Childlessness Report'. It would add to these for discussion within the Church the following issues raised by the Committee of Inquiry in its Report:

(a) Pastoral concern for childless couples;
(b) The priority that should be accorded, within medical provision, to the childless and to infertility research and treatment;
(c) Embryo research and questions about the status and rights of the embryo;
(d) The influence of technology on the shaping of attitudes.

(In submitting its statement, the Board has been glad to associate itself on certain matters of detail with discussions of the British Council of Churches and Free Church Federal Council.)'

Appendix 2

BOARD OF SOCIAL RESPONSIBILITY
Deliverance of the General Assembly of the Church of Scotland on the Report of the Board of Social Responsibility.

At Edinburgh, the twentieth day of May, One thousand nine hundred and eighty-six years —

The General Assembly:
1 Receive the Report of the Board of Social Responsibility and thank the Convener and Vice-Conveners, Sub-Committee Conveners, and members of the Board, Executive and Office Staff, Field Work and Residential Staff.
2 Recognising the increasing social and spiritual problems of the long-term unemployed, encourage the Board to bring to the next General Assembly firm proposals for ameliorating such problems.
3 Welcome the Board's clear policy of development in four main areas — senile dementia, mental handicap, mental illness, misuse of alcohol and drugs — and the considerable efforts to obtain appropriate funding.
4 Approve the report on work with the elderly, and commend the Board for the development of its work for people with senile dementia.
5 Commend the considerable changes in the work of Community Care; acknowledge with gratitude the contribution of staff in areas of work now discontinued; and congratulate the Board for its initiative and industry in developing a number of significant new projects.
6 Express concern at the withdrawal of Central Government funding for training, and commend the Board for seeking to continue the necessary training programme.
7 Note the Report on finance and funding and commend the Board's initiatives to maximise funding available for the care of people in need.
8 Note with concern the setting up of a factory to manufacture oral tobacco products (Skoal Bandits) and the promotion and introduction of these products into the community. Further express concern that HM Government is prepared to afford financial support in the form of Regional Development Grants, believed to amount to £1 000 000 to assist the multi-national corporation involved to build their factory which produces yet another harmful tobacco product.
9 Endorse the Report of the Study Group of the Study Group on Alcohol and Drugs, and encourage its discussion by Presbyteries and congregations of the Church.
10 Recall Section 19 of the Deliverance of last General Assembly on the Board's Report except for the words — 'The General Assembly receive the report on abortion'; reaffirm the position held since 1966, that the criteria for abortion

should be that the continuance of the pregnancy would involve serious risk to the life or grave injury to the health whether physical or mental, of the pregnant woman; and instruct the Board to seek a review of the working of the 1967 Abortion Act, with a view to the eradication of any laxity in its interpretation.

11 While noting the interim reports of the Committee on Health and Healing and the Study Group on Abortion and that fuller reports on these subjects will be presented to the 1987 General Assembly, instruct, as a matter of urgency, that the report on abortion will be a re-examination, with fuller research and wider consultation, of the question of abortion and in particular the inviolability of the fetus.

12 Express concern that obstetricians and gynaecologists opposed to abortion are effectively being excluded from posts at Senior Registrar and Consultant level, and instruct the Board to investigate, to make appropriate representations to Health Boards and Her Majesty's Government, with a view to effective implementation of the 'conscience clause' in the 1967 Abortion Act, and to report to the General Assembly of 1986.

13 Note the report of the Lifestyle Survey, and urge Presbyteries and congregations to study the final report when available and to act on the questions which it raises with regard to moral, social and spiritual issues affecting the Christians witness and the future life of the Church.

14 Recognise the continuing importance of the Women's Council to the Work of the Board, and the contribution of Local Committees.

3.3 Study Group on Abortion

The Study Group on Abortion is continuing its examination of issues raised for the Church by the matter of abortion. In seeking to carry forward this work, members of the Study Group are engaged in consultation with a number of individuals and have studied the comments received from various sources within the Church as important contributions to their on-going work. The Study Group is concerned in particular with pastoral issues in this area, and will report in full to the General Assembly in 1987.